THE DOTS WILL NOT BE JOINED is a snapshot into sport, life, coaching, art, philosophy, from a bloke who doesn't accept that things are linear – that we have to see, read, understand in straight lines. It's a brilliant and rich memoir but not that well-behaved. It's about now and it's clamouring for the imagination. It credits you, the public, with the capacity to think; to carry more than just the one, predictable narrative forward.

There are **football** and **cricket** things but also ruminations on how and why we judge and what makes us judge. It's already being viewed as a cult classic. This short, (s)punky book has more ideas and more style and more guts than most epic novels. Oh – and it will make you smile.

Don't get angsty about *what it is*: it may be nothing, it may be the first part of a three or thirty-three part autobiography. It may just be asking questions.

Cover photo of Rick Walton (Everton reserve kit) and eldest bro' Chris from about 1968; probably taken by Keith Winston Walton, also known as Dad.

Rear cover pic of Victor Edward Dodsworth, ex Doncaster Rovers, Grimsby Town and Manchester United. 'Grandpa'/The Mighty Vic. Photographer unknown.

The bowlingatvincent multi-national
corporation brings you

THE DOTS WILL NOT
BE JOINED.

(Football. Cricket. *Stories*.)

*To ALEX & GOODIE
WITH LOVE (& APOLOGIES TO
THE TOTTINGHAM FAN).*

♡   Rick

BY
RICK WALTON

Grosvenor House
Publishing Limited

This book is published by
Grosvenor House Publishing Ltd
Link House
140 The Broadway, Tolworth, Surrey, KT6 7HT.
www.grosvenorhousepublishing.co.uk

A CIP record for this book
is available from the British Library

ISBN 978-1-83975-792-1

This is a Compendium of Ideas.
Warning: contains mischief.

CONTENTS

"I know the highest and the best / I afford them all due respect / But the brightest jewel inside of me / Glows with pleasure at my own stupidity".

Song from Under the Floorboards. MAGAZINE.

ACKNOWLEDGEMENTS.

COVER and REAR COVER ARTWORK by the Diamond Geezer Himself, Mr Kevin Little – kevin@ kevinlittlecreative.com

With thanks to Al and Susannah and, inevitably, apologies for not listening to *everything*.

Hearty handshake to all who have supported/tolerated/ faked it convincingly via the Twitters or in real life – whatever that is. This nobody really is nobody without you.

Special mention to a lard-arsed bloke outta Leeds, who claims to be Duncan McKenzie's cousin. You've carried me through, ya mad, wounded, giant-bastard, with your music and heart. Thanks, too, to the other GY Whatsapp Soulbro's; **the finest blokes I know.**

Pintabeer, or worse, to the fella Ronay: in my opinion the most brilliant and imaginative scribbler out there. Ridiculous and weirdly humbling to have someone *that fabulous* - someone I've never met – so graciously agree to write a foreword on my behalf, knowing that there's no dosh and probably no kudos in it for him.

The fact that the Euros and the Olympics so ungraciously intervened in no way diminishes my thanks. Genuinely.

The late, Grealish-like sub for Barney R was Paul Mason: I know, decent, eh? Cheating, in the sense that Paul has been a mate for years but a) another Giant Talent and b) an outstanding contributor to contemporary political/cultural/philosophical life. So c) I don't stress too much about the notion that the bloke from Leigh has my back a little. He has things to say and they tend to be worth listening to. Paul, grateful simply does not cover it.

Finally, thanks to the kids, coaches, teachers, players, punks and bloody inspiring people who have populated the stories so far. Plus family and mates from early days, who fleshed-out the games and the ways that made me. You other folks... well, grab a ball and join us next time out.

Rick.

FOREWORD – by Paul Mason.

'Write like you speak' is meant to be the first commandment of journalism. But in sports journalism it's usually the last. Stabbing away at the laptop, during the final seconds of a big game, hacks on deadline reach for cliche after cliche, deftly making the case for the rapid introduction of artificial intelligence.

This is sports writing of a different kind. If Neville Cardus had somehow collaborated with Jack Kerouac, they might have produced what Rick Walton does here.

He writes like he speaks, weaving moral philosophy with cricket coaching tips, digressing into autobiography and genealogy, just as he might do while casting a rod for mackerel off the cliffs of Pembrokeshire, or heaving through the crowds for Wales vs France on a rainy Cardiff evening.

In Walton's writing "truth and hierarchy are subverted... they are Morecambe and Wise retreating to the distance with that daft but somehow poignant dance". In their place, he resurrects what he sees as the key - not just to sporting greatness but to life - freedom, spontaneity, self-belief. Noticing rather than explaining.

Unleashed from structure, Walton ranges from the ethics of Maradona's hand to the thermodynamics of swing bowling to memoirs of following Grimsby Town in the days of flares and sideburns.

At the centre of his philosophy - because that's what this is, and it's no more aphoristic than Nietzsche - lies the concept of "unweighting": what the batter at cricket has to do to achieve poise and mercuriality in the face of fast bowling. For Walton, almost everything in sport is about unweighting your mind from rules, doubts, corporate obligations, and the pressure hierarchies that surround them.

This is a year when top-tier sportsmen and women, from tennis to cricket to gymnastics, have faced up to their mental health issues openly, fought back against the corporate and media pressures placed on them, and embraced the potential of sport as a political force for good.

So it's refreshing to take a dip into Walton's wild world, where none of it really matters except the joy of playing; the connection of the physical body with mental self-belief; sport as a game for creating indelible memories of goodness.

PREAMBLE.

Retaliation? In first.

You will soon see, friends, that this is wildish, in execution. Possibly too blog-like, possibly too self-obsessed to be taken seriously as a book. I've spent more time than you will imagine thinking on this and trying to nudge it all closer towards Proper Volume-dom and intelligibility but you may not accept this to be either fact or mitigation. I don't want or expect you to. I'd like you please to read The Dots Will Not Be Joined and see how it strikes.

This is a journal, a soul-search in to sport and a statement of faith. Because I absolutely grew up through football and have now coached cricket for a living for ten years.[1] Because I am besotted with the idea that these daft games – or our capacity to enjoy or indulge in movement and common purpose – are massively wonderful and massively important. Consequently we will wade through stories together, many of which I hope you will recognise, though the dates, stats, protagonists may shuffle. The hope is, in sharing larks both trivial and profound, that questions are asked about what forms us.

---

[1] Community Cricket Coach, for Cricket Wales.

There's no avoiding that much of this is personal and that *my way* might feel a challenge or an indulgence. Forgive me. Stick with it. Forget the rules – maybe particularly the ones about penmanship. Hah! It is implicit here that the gilded gates to publishing have been breached by an insolent outsider. There is mischief around that but we get to cricket and football soon enough.

My volunteering at a cricket club turned into work, ten years ago. Writing has been happening since the year dot: it turned into two blogs then, extraordinarily, into the wonderful indulgence that has been ECB Accreditation. Coupla Wisden mentions later and I am still an absolute nobody but an emboldened one: happy to write how I write.

To this feral soul the world does seem unhinged and dreamy and colorific; so hard to compute all this elegant erudition elsewhere. Why the ordered lawns, the bookishness? I don't get it – in fact I *oppose it.*

So yes, this is a medium-untamed contribution - a Compendium of Ideas. With too many 'I's. Lacking shelf-life. Often about judgements. Often eyebrow-raisingly speculative.

Hoping some of it feels true.

Rick.

ONE - CONVOLUTION.

This is a lop-sided relationship from the start. Maybe most are? Maybe life is full of situations where you have to or need to recognise hierarchy, or folks suggest that you do. Otherwise chaos, dysfunction or – god forbid – radicalism.

But hey, let's not get too politico-philosophical too early, eh? Other than to say that despite being a medium-ancient white geezer, I'm okay with challenge, individual genius and the spark of life, goddammit, that may come from bypassing, defying or even disrespecting 'structures'. Therefore, when I am teacher, my default position *has* to be an awareness that your brilliance, your freedom, your magnificent contribution (dear student) could be the way to go, to win, to make the world better. Me being the writer here is more inconsequentially inevitable than reflective of sources of knowledge or authority.

Apologies if we're already convoluted. That may not change and why would it, when the world is so wonderfully labyrinthine *and its appeal is, too*?

If, in lurching forward, we *did choose* to limit our considerations to those around sport then the answer to pretty much every question imaginable might remain similarly knotty: everything "depends". Decisions and the execution thereof are so contingent on what's happening in the game/in your head/with your colleagues or the opposition, that we really can get lost in (or hide behind?) the four zillion variables. And yet somehow things turn out to be exhilaratingly simple so often *'if you can but see your way'*. Speaking as sportsman and coach, I find that beguiling, beautiful bastard of a conundrum intoxicating.

*

Before we get into any tenuous, Waltonian view of how and why things happen, allow me to clear my throat, nail my colours, hoist my petard. This will not be a self-help book or some other capitulation to orthodoxy. It will not seek to channel you towards corporate thinking and I hope and expect it will steer clear of allied language or assumptions around How We Should Really Do Stuff. I can and will occasionally ride the swell of my own pomp – forgive me – but always, always I invite you to take this as seriously as you bloody like. Given that we all surely revel in the bantziness, the mischief of the universe, just call out any cobblers; roll round in it, giggling, legs in the air, avec Yours F Truly. I have some opinions and even some expertise: mainly I am gloriously and hilariously unsure.

Oh, and did I say, this is really not just about sport? I am struck by the notion – ill-understood but constantly there – that the times are so crazy and febrile that there is something of an obligation, *at every opportunity,* to offer some rallying-cry towards thoughtfulness, goodness, honesty. Because maybe everything needs to defy not just the opposites, but also blandness, conciliation with dumb prejudice and the drift into apathy. So how could anything 'just be about sport?' I make no apology for the whiff of ethicality, here, but please don't go mistaking that for conservatism – I think it's the opposite.

*

In a cynical universe there is a huge danger that we Tweeps and you Instas rush to **judge everything**: plainly we are driven to do so by a deliberately subverted technoverse, where outrage feeds The Machine.[2] In my feeble attempt to re-balance all this bawling, some unsubtle campaigning (of a sort) may creep in to this meandering epistle. Again, take it as seriously as you like: with global players of a distinctly unsporting nature manipulating our ability or will to unpick arguments or step outside the narrative of click/get data-raped/buy, somebody has to scream a little. Scream or – as Munch did - actually mount that crazy-high horse of defiant, expressive, committed, soul-stirring rumination.

(For clarity; not remotely comparing myself with Edvard Munch[3] - lols! Our horses are on ver-ry different courses. Just merely saying we're entitled to rage both

---

[2] It's by no means my only source, here but Julia Bell's laceratingly brilliant 'Radical Attention' fleshes out the argument... go see.

[3] Edvard Munch, Norwegian expressionist painter and advocate for the soul – most famously responsible for 'The Scream'.

inside and out at the pornographic baseness of much public/political/philosophical parley).

So yeh; gonna 'range', here, unashamedly. Across sport, morality, philosophy, arts. And the dots will most definitely not be joined.

TWO - YEH BUT IS IT REAL, THOUGH?

How, indeed, in the time of nil attention span, can any of us be sure of the meaning, depth, place, truth of anything? How can we be so certain and so **right** when, for example... *this?*

*

You are in the stomach-tightening whirlwind of a Really Big Match. (Or it feels that way). Everything is **on you.** You want to win, you want to make people happy and proud but if you're honest you also want it to be over – it's so crushing, this moment. And yet you're plain wrong: possibly.

Why wrong? Because there are those who make the case for pressure simply not being real, being a construct, something we build in our minds; something we may more or less capitulate to when sense/atmosphere/occasion trigger an understanding that this is Squeaky Bum Time. But how wonderful, how *empowering* might it be if we could recognise that understanding as a fraud? As a misunderstanding; as a roguish devil on-the-shoulder; a distraction.

*

Rich Hudson, Managing Director, Bucks Cricket, Level 4 Coach, Performance Psychologist, writer, thinker and ver ver interesting twitterer @rdhudson00, says something to the effect that pressure is just thoughts that waft in. (Writing this, yes, I am deliberately owning my calumny of a low-grade précis. This is dense, fascinating stuff and I am inevitably going to dangle dumb baubles all over it. Forgive me, move on and make the assumption that I'm trying *not* to traduce every essential part. I rate the guy).

Rich means, I suppose, that because there is *nothing actually there* - we merely engineered stuff - we are able or theoretically able to make choices or interventions which may re-shape the psychological moment and claw back control.

*

Let's try a couple of what tend to get called 'scenarios': a word that's becoming so ubiquitous in sports development-speak that I may yet scribble it out. A word that though it may be suitable and even inevitable given the environment, is proper excruciating - like environment.

Anyway, firstly you are coaching an Under 11 cricket team, hosting a general discussion about batting, probably at a training session. Maybe you have asked the question *so how do we feel, what's going on, when the wicket falls that means you're walking out there, next?*

Often players might take a few seconds to respond to this. Fair enough. Likely if the team is boys (did you assume that?) there may be a bit of jostling to be the last to (shock, horror) open up to any weakness or fear. Or it could be that my assumption of a certain level of reticence around young males offering out their potential anxieties is cobblers... and they pour it all out. If not, you ask again – you prompt.

What's been going on, inside you, for the last whatever – ten minutes, twenty minutes?

They know you're talking about nerves so somebody will probably say something about 'butterflies'. Then more, from other players.

If you're like me you really want to plant something fairly significant about this into their heads; something about energy and confidence and control. You also both really want to get into speechifying... and know that you shouldn't. Hold your tongue. Wait for them to trip out more ideas.

*

Skip forward two minutes. Half of what they've said is overheard coach-bilge they think you want them to re-spew, bless 'em, but there is some meaningful thinking and expression going on. It strikes you again that your job might be to both acknowledge that and hopefully to make it intelligible – then take it forward.

Without over-egging it, this can be an important intervention, whether you break out your Churchillian gears or engage Quietly Reassuring Mode. We're all different: more on this later, probably.

However, you **need to make it work** (that's part of your responsibility as coach, yes?) because

a)   these walking-out-to-bat moments are MASSIVE in cricket
b)   your experience is that many players underachieve, in these SBTs[4] and
c)   because maybe you personally *fire up* under the knowledge that you might **clear something** or even inspire these callow youths, right here, right now, if you judge your audience well. And that's magic.

*

Hey I'm not sure if you have to quote Rich Hudson, Carl Jung or Stormzy at this juncture but it may be that it's appropriate and valuable, even, to offer the following, or something similar, to nudge this on.

Right. We've agreed that there are these feelings, before we walk out. Maybe particularly if they've got a demon fast bowler? What's that all about?

---

[4]   Squeaky Bum Time – after Alex Ferguson, dumbo!

More discussion. You try to gently unpick and/or focus. Then

O-kaaay so we're agreeing that we're pooping our panties, just a little, when that moment comes. You walk out to bat. So let's think about strategies - don't like that word much either, but kids are getting comfortable with it, via school and clubs - *strategies that might see us through towards the outcome that we might want. Incidentally what is it that we all want?*

You might get some great answers here, hopefully a laugh or two, if matey boy (your quick bowler?) says "fifty not out!" and the skipper says "dream on, pal", precipitating major #bantz and giggles. Conversely it really may be a surprisingly reflective moment. Enjoy any laughs: move on.

*How about this? Rich Hudson, a writer, sports psychologist and expert on how our heads work looks at moments like these in this way. He says in effect that there **is no pressure**. Repeat: Is. No. Pressure.*

It's what boffins might call a construct... because it isn't real... it's something we feel but it is nothing more than a bundle of thoughts fluttering away – like butterflies.

Let's say that again. That feeling, that gut-churning feeling you get, that most of us get walking out to face that first ball is made of nothing. And therefore if we can get our head around that, we really might be able to block it out, train ourselves, maybe, to completely dismiss the negatives, the fears that undermine us as we *prepare to walk out and bat. And remember batting is something that most of us **love to do!** Or certainly hitting the ball is something that we love to do, so it's probably criminal that we let something spoil that, undermine that so easily.*

How great would it be to call out that pressure – call it fake, call it bollocks, call it a completely harmless cloud of nothing?

Imagine what your batting would be like if you hadn't leaked all that energy freaking out before you trudged to the wicket, or during those first couple of overs.

*

After this we/you can talk about **how** individuals might call out the fraud that is pressure. Can you blank it out in the conceptual way described above? (Could most eleven-year-olds?) Even if the answer to both those questions is yes – and I have pret-ty profound doubts – maybe it's helpful to talk through alternative or supporting strategies?

I have been known to offer the idea of Conscious Breaths,[5] drawn from yoga. I am a stiff old git and a shockingly amateur exponent/participant in yoga but I definitely drop into a few ujjayi breaths to compose

---

[5] Conscious Breaths/ujjayi breaths are a way of drawing in to the moment, into the experience of breathing and thereby excluding clutter and distraction. They facilitate real calm.

myself when the need arises. (I might do this consciously, or automatically, if any of that makes sense?)

One possible extension of this discussion – which needs revisiting, yes? - is to ask the players to think about what they do in this moment... and what they *might do*. Maybe you set that as 'homework?' Or maybe it feels fine to keep going without a break? Judge your audience. Are folks engaged, or are you pontificating?

Of course if we're talking cricket or sport – and possibly now might be the time to air the thought that these ideas *may* have applications outside of an Under 11 cricket match – then we prepare physically, too, to move well and therefore 'compete'.

In fact, traditionally, it feels like most of what we do or have done is to contemplate the physical. It's only in recent years that we coaches have gone all wusstastically soft and thought about mindset. Great coaches may always have been sensitive to the human frailties of their players but I'm not sure psychology/mindset was really factored in – or not overtly, not discussed openly – until (crazy-guess) about the year 2000. Life before then was largely Neanderthal; men were men who gritted it out. So were women.

Ordinarily (ha! What the hell does that mean?) coaches and players would be into thinking about a **ready position:** 'set-up' or stance. We'd be thinking about balance and concentration and coordinated movements. Maybe critically, before that first ball we'd be thinking about what we now call trigger movements, all the things you do to **unweight yourself**[6] and facilitate your counter to the bowler. These are major not-to-say seminal moments where grooving and technical skills meet a potentially bloody intimidating 'cherry'. Not going there in any depth, right now. In conclusion, going back into the mind games. To Jos Buttler and, with apologies, Scenario Two.

*

Jos Buttler is one of the UK's most talented sportsmen. Wicketkeeper-batsman for England (and Wales): has what have traditionally been described as 'outrageous gifts' - fabulous phrase, that!

In short, it's his batting that is remarkable; for its flair, inventiveness and sheer, glorious cheek. Buttler is a leading exponent of the modern art of dismissing, gliding, flipping and driving the ball to and beyond the boundary, in ways that still may secretly outrage the dino-toffs amongst the MCC[7] Membership. You may not know that there really has been a revolution going on in cricket over recent years – arguably more than one. Buttler, whilst remaining outwardly quietish, articulate and charming, even, is one of the flashy musketeers at the centre of this riot.

---

[6] More on this later but 'unweighting' is a concept around freeing up the body (specifically) to prepare it to face fast bowling. Extraordinarily, the great Aussie intellectual Ian Chappell delivered this into the coaching arena... and it's a proper beaut.

[7] Marylebone Cricket Club. A soft target but an extraordinarily privileged posse – and therefore ahem, conservative.

*

Let's strip the world temporarily of the Pressure-Deniers – like that Hudson fella. Let's describe in all innocence the illustrious patriarchy that is the Normal World, in which Jos Buttler plies his mischievous trade. Normally Ar Jos strides out in front of many thousands of salivating blokes who expect him to deliver. And normally they *ache* for that because the Blokes Before Jos (in Tests, notably) were shite. The ether is loaded with angst, expectation and alcohol and the match is loaded against him.

(Actually, given that as I write England – Men - are World Champions in the 50 Over format and ver-ry tasty at T20, this is a travesty. But it contains more than a little truth, given the sense that Buttler - and Stokes, possibly, in particular - have often yomped out to the crease with the proverbial 'job to do').

Buttler walks out to take guard with the words "fuck it" etched into the top of his bat handles. As an emancipatory motif? To shape his context? To de-mystify or de-bunk what, exactly?

*

This is one of the more striking manifestations of something I may be about to call #psychobantz. (Let it go: it's what I do). But what is it? It smacks more of a soft-left, post-hippie perspectivism than rank machismo or competitive rage. It answers the yammering crowd and the ominous moment with liberatingly laconic brass.

This was all a joyously secretive personal reminder until TV cameras picked it up when Buttler scored a match-winning 80 against Pakistan, at Headingley, in the summer of 2020. When asked what the eff this was all about, he said

"I think it's just something that reminds me of what my best mindset is – when I'm playing cricket, and probably in life as well…

It puts cricket in perspective. When you nick off, does it really matter?"

Setting aside any 'concern' about language – c'mon, in 2021 COVID, Alt-rightism, racism, sexism and homophobia are issues, right, not swear-words? - this eff-it **is interesting**. Some might say it's refreshing, others exciting and positive. I'm personally not aware of *anybody* who thinks it's a Bad Thing. (That in itself is interesting, yes?)

Everybody likes that Buttler scribbles those two words on his bats: I believe he was doing it to all of them and I'm not clear if the authorities have now intervened. Whatever. Everybody liked it. But again, what was it that he was doing? What was it **aimed at?**

Clearly he's defying stuff. Pressure? The Authorities? Fear? Conservatism? This is rich, abstract territory so probably all of those things.

*

My reading of this wonderfully layered story is that he's maybe not doing the whole conceptual denial-thing that Rich Hudson has posited as one helpful response to those incoming, performance-subverting butterflies. Buttler is calling out to perspective, to Bigger Things, rather than denying the very existence of pressure. He's freeing himself up to have a larf, despite the alleged presence of that which might tend to constrain him (or anybody else). To quantify the patently unmeasurable – we do that, right? – I'd say he's maybe 80% towards puritanical anti-pressuredom.

In doing this, whilst batting for Ingerland, having returned to the Test side after an eighteen-month gap, it feels somehow like Buttler was flicking the vees for all of us. We all want to find a way to be free – or more free.

THREE - SUNSHINE ON LEITH?

There's much more to be said about #psychobantz, plainly. Like everything else, I think we can say it both with a twinkle of mischief *and* a genuine dollop of respect and appreciation. Newness is exciting, challenging and nourishing. Thinking is good.

Performance Psychology is a whole new industry in much the same way that Sport Development itself is. I am close enough to both culture-zones to be both supportive of the progressive nature of their missions – Jeez, another horrendously ubiquitous word, commandeered by The Corporates - and a wee bit concerned about the indulgences they may imply. Ditto Strength and Conditioning.

(Urgent insert: nobody with more than three brain-cells is going to dismiss any of the above out of hand. However, despite knowing fabulous people of real integrity in all three fields, I'm happy to place the notion before you that elite sport in particular may be becoming over-loaded with Assistant Coaches. Folks who need to be consulted. Folks who need to justify their existence. Without being a cheap controversialist, I predict a slimming-down, in time, of - for example - international cricket coaching groups. *And/or,* more freelancing and short-term consultancy).

This sounds a whole lot more cynical than I feel: gonna leave it in, because I think there may be a grain of truth enclosed. Consider it a friendly contention, not a slight on three entirely legitimate and honourable professions.

*

But back to that Under 11s scenario: briefly. Because this is my book – na-ncr-na-ner-ner – I'm going to sling in what I might have said (and probably have said) about the approach to that extraordinary sporting moment – the 'getting in' thing, in cricket.

I think this whole thing about butterflies is magic. The fact that nearly all of us, in our different ways – whether we're Joe Bloggs or Jos Buttler – experience something similar, when walking out, taking guard, playing that first ball or those first couple of overs. It's magic.

What if we accept that the nerves are just our bodies saying to us "COME ON?!? Let's 'ave i-it!!" What if it's just some incredible energy coursing through us? **Energy we can use?** *How about if we look to* **turn that energy into concentration?**

For me there is a way to feel that buzz – those butterflies – and divert that charge into really intense concentration... on the ball. Use the power. Channel that surge... towards the ball. As the bowler approaches... make sure you're unweighted, you're ready, your feet are ready to dance... but that **you are concentrated.**

I think these moments in cricket are amongst the most wonderful and challenging in sport. To 'overcome your nerves' in these few minutes is to burst through into something truly satisfying.

I'm not a particularly sentimental bloke but I do hold onto some pret-ty poignant memories around conversions of this nature: folks in your care *growing*. It does happen – it has happened. 'Scuse me whilst I grab a large glass of Cabalié, stare mistily at the curtains and select "Sunshine On Leith"[8] on my Spotify.

*

As a coach, even at my feeble level, it feels bloody marvellous to be able to support players across this delicious but sometimes acutely painful terrain. We all know people who cannot get through: I'm thinking right now about a really good young player from one of my regional groups who was so hamstrung by fear – particularly of fast bowlers – that he would cry off from certain fixtures. We all know individuals like him, in sport, in life, who find it impossible to overcome these obstacles *at particular times*. This young guy I gave plenty of slack. He was ten or eleven when he ducked out: he is now twenty-odd and one of the best young all-rounders in our area.

---

[8] Wonderfully melancholic number from folkie-punkie Scots duo The Proclaimers. Beautiful, tender and triumphant in that quiet, soulful, modest way you very rarely find. Drink some whisky and have a good old blub.

INTER-CHAPTER – scratch-mix/ sub/Maradona.

Sound superfluous, or just arrogant, if I drop in now that a fabulous woman I loved and respected described me as an 'honourable anarchist?' (She didn't quite mean it literally but I'm happy with what she captured – or what I understand from it). Think of it as a Profile Pic: it may even help.

*

But hang on. Can feel some of you – and certainly anybody who Writes Stuff – bristling. When, precisely, am I going to deign to inform you, or give you some kindof idea what the hell this book is all about? Well... soonish – and when I know. There *will be* anarchy; I warned you. **The dots will not be joined.**

*

Because I *receive life* as a crazy-wunnerful kaleidoscope, and because I know that the football hooligans I grew up with had talent, wit and value, so it can only be that truth and hierarchy are utterly, beautifully, mischievously subverted. Necessarily so. T and H are mutable: we can twinkle at them. They are Morecambe and Wise retreating to the distance with that daft but somehow poignant dance. They are Ben Stokes switch-hitting for six. They are stories. They are four-year-olds (or me, or you) in the presence of Rothko.

*

So, in this smörgåsbord[9] of mirages, meaning and nebulous mischief does the fact that *I'm writing* offer some credence to what I'm going to say? *Yes and no.*

Will there be answers here? *Doubt it.*

Is this whole thing about luxuriating in the richness of our challenges? *Too right!*

Is it okay to be 'disproportionate', because the questions feel urgent, even when they palpably aren't? *TOO RIGHT!*

Ok good. Maybe we understand each other. Let's crack on: Maradona.

---

[9] Yup. In there for a bet.

FOUR – DEVIL ON MY SHOULDER.

It's very much on the record that there were TWO Maradonas. Diego and the football god. The former was a lovely, honest urchin – or that's how we in the Civilised West have harvested him. It may be true, or largely so: it may also be a kind of projection, borne of our arrogance. Seems fair to accept that he came from poverty and narrow possibilities; that his freakishly beautiful communion with a football was 'his only way out'. My god, how he took it. My god – how it took him!

*

Diego was thrust simultaneously into a suffocating tunnel and an unrestrained Carnival of Opportunity. Fearsome family responsibilities and a sex-and-drugs fest. The slum, the sunshine, the glory, the Camorra. Maradona got the trophies, got made and got warped.

But questions. Was he a kind of fauve artist – and therefore *relatively* free from damnation, cos 'talented' - merely following the prototype of flawed, sexualised genius? Does the misogyny and the drug mis-use matter, (or how much does it matter), in the context of the tectonic achievement that was Napoli[10] and the inevitable combustion of a Soul Unable to Cope? How can responsibilities and achievements be measured, in a case where there is such phenomenal gift, such coercion, such drudgery? Who the hell was around Diego, when it mattered?

*

Who *was* around Diego when he was hulking into Maradona? Not just in those later years, when the low-slung genius morphed into Dwarf Elvis? Was it ever possible that The Fall (if that's what it was) could have been cushioned by some life-saving, career-saving, fire-blanket-wielding mentor? Or is the whole point about Maradona that he fed off all that edginess and *could never be reached?* Is that what happens, to artists? To Jackson Pollock and Vincent van Gogh; to Amy Winehouse, Dylan Thomas... and Gazza?

*

Take the wild associations as seriously as you like: is there any way to explain where unthinkable artistry comes from? *Do we undermine the romance at the heart of this, if we seek to make sense of it?* Do duffers like me, who can't help wonder what a quiet word might have done, need to leave the Maradona Legacy in

---

[10] Maradona lifted rough-and-tumble, 'barely Italian' city of Napoli – hated or viewed with contempt by Romans and the Northern Giants Juventus and AC and Inter Milan - to two Serie A titles. He became a coke-addled, perverse, irresistible god.

peace? And what reconciles that surge in my heart when I think of how he moved, what he did, with those prosaic enquiries?

I saw Maradona play live, just the once. Wembley, 1980. (Ten fascinating minutes of YouTube highlights available, via Bing Video. England 3 Argentina 1. Go see?)

My memory is that we didn't really know – not yet - who this guy was. We were football people but the sense in the crowd was unmistakably laced with some incredulity when he raced away from three England defenders before flipping the ball with the outside of that left foot towards Clemence's right-hand post. It was ver-ry nearly as wondrous as his eye-popping World Cup goal (the one after that Hand of God moment), only the ball shaved the outside of the upright, with Phil Neal, Dave Watson and the rest gawping stupidly in his wake.

There were flashes of irresistible genius that night, during a high-octane encounter won by England with two goals from David Johnson and one from Keegan, countered by an emphatic pen from Passarella. (Maradona had won the spot-kick with another sinuous burst into the box. He may have fallen somewhat theatrically over Sansom's tame challenge but the full-back had been beaten. The home crowd didn't like it much but we knew this lad-with-the-thighs deserved something).

Looking back, I smile to think of Diego jinking and racing towards (and past!) Dave Watson, the hugely honest but relatively limited England stopper. Once, in midfield, Maradona having done a classic swivel and roadrunner number on him, Watson clattered the Argentinian about a calendar month late. It was almost funny: like the Sunday League mis-match where the forty-year-old stopper cynically wallops the opposition's darting front-man – the flyer, bit flash and back from uni' - before scowling 'not so clever now, pal'. In the stands we may have smiled, with relief as much as malice. But more generously, I do recall a number of occasions where thousands of us home supporters offered up our hands – alongside the expletives – when their number ten rendered the un-bloody-believable exhilaratingly real.

*

What can you do, with genius? And what *is it* – apart from being a reason to live?

The Maradona Story feels familiar even to those who aren't football fans. This has to do with both visibility and inevitable tragedy, for sure, but *what is* the extra dimension in play, here? What are and how come, those gifts?

FIVE – STATMAAN!!

Coaches make judgements. We all do. Excuse the hyperbole but how and why we choose, decide or select and the balance (or battle?) between intuition, knowledge and information received, in the period leading up to that call, is somewhere between compelling and outright spellbinding. As well as demanding.

In mid-ponder, recently, it suddenly dawned that there's something **I love** about selecting teams, as well as leading groups of players. Of course the two things very often go together, but somehow this particular *separation* of the roles – or my identification of specific feelings about dovetailing duties - had somehow previously failed to register. This has got me thinking about all the times when I've ever thought (or said) something like *'Jesus. Never noticed that before'*. Because, well why, given that I've been involved with selecting teams for thirty-something years, did this happen now?

*

Could be this book is more about noticing than explaining. (Bit like how Proper Yoga is about awareness more than movement, maybe?) Not too concerned whether that is a strength or a weakness... or perceived as such. I do not know *why I just realised that I love picking teams. On.*

*

My sudden micro-recognition may simply be another pointer towards the following factoid: that coaching is massive and multi-dimensional and – sorry, one of my favourite words – **rich**. It's intoxicatingly challenging. It gets personal, it gets nasty. You have to isolate *and* integrate stuff. You have to be tough *and* sensitive. You have to train and coach. It's wonderful.

Back to the *judgements, specifically.* Good selection (which might in itself be appraised under an extraordinary range of criteria, yes?) does not arise, necessarily from the same bank of knowledge and experience as say, Strength and Conditioning. Obviously. Neither is it the same as the ability to impart game intelligence, or captaincy skills. It may not imply a facility for diplomacy: it may not even suggest that you, as leader, are a man or woman to be followed – not necessarily. Both sharp, narrow things and voluptuous complexities are juggling, here.

We can all think of coaches or managers, at professional or recreational level, who just 'have something' authentic and compelling. In short, you and/or the players believe in them. How they made it to that Special Place is something I ask you to further contemplate. Meanwhile I'm going on with selection.

*

There is something about that responsibility – which I take very seriously – that feels both spiky and humbling but also deeply energising. Selecting teams at any level is a real privilege: it matters to players and families because they want to win. It matters equally to your Twelfth (Wo)men, substitutes, reserves or bench, who want to know that a) they're not forgotten and b) that there's a chance a-coming. It matters that you keep the *blend on the pitch* right but also the relationships on the fringes healthy. This is tough, at every level. Deciding is difficult.

How we make decisions is changing – or rather in professional sport, it is. And this is already having an influence on us jokers down the pecking order. Why? Technology, in a word. The implications of exponential increase of available knowledge: which is to say, laptops and cameras.

*

One of the eighty-four revolutions currently going on in pro' cricket is around statistics. Earnest young men (mainly) are recording the detail of nearly everything, to facilitate strategies based upon strengths, weaknesses, likelihoods. Very recently (2020 Indian Premier League) and not without some controversy, live computations have been flagged out to participants from coded boards in the coaching area, so as to guide players on what the implications of this or that are, or to tell them specifically to clout the living daylights out of the spinner in the next over. This is merely and inevitably **sharp franchises** seeking those marginal gains: you know, the ones that worked so well for our friends at TEAM SKY. It's just another kind of algorithmning.

'Analysis' is a thing: explosively so, in cricket. It's a radical change: now, every county, country and (maybe particularly?) short-format outfit sees stats as central to selection and strategy.

*

The repercussions are wide-ranging and fascinating. They certainly affect the role and the power-base of the coach and may include ethical concerns – around accuracy, interpretation, fairness – as well as issues of player-ownership and initiative. (Could players become so reliant on the lap counters that they forget how to drive? What risks - ironically - of poor interpretation undermining any potential benefits?)

My interest in this, or rather my *position* might, I concede, be a generational thing, me being more Bothamesque (age-wise, not politically) than Buttleresque. If, alongside this Stat Goldrush, players are forever looking to the stands for their strategies, then something may be lost. In any case, my hunch is that most athletes don't want too much information. They want to express. The stroppy ones – bless 'em - may ignore the signals and play 'by instinct'.

*

Two signature motifs across sports, in recent years, are power transfer and Sports Science. The latter is arguably such an enormous field that anything I park in this chapter is going to feel insultingly inadequate. What I hope to do is to point – again, more gleefully than ironically – towards some of the rich contradictions and fascinations arising from new intelligence.

*

It's not just in cricket that the power shift, placing players (back?) at the centre, has been striking. For a decade or so you haven't been able to go anywhere near sport generally without hearing stuff about 'player-centredness'. I even wrote something myself for the ECB Coaching Association mag, on precisely that subject. 'Yes but what does it all mean?' (For #ECB #Coaching Insight; also available on cricketmanwales.com).

Philosophically this adjustment in cricket Coach Ed was about enshrining the rights of the player and an understanding of what was appropriate *for them* at the heart of their experience. 'Core Principles' - that is, relatively open areas of guidance, as opposed to fixed expectation – became the way. It was a strong reminder to us coaches to put away our egos and listen; to lead less by directing and demonstrating and more by asking great questions along a road to discovery. Very 21st century, very generous and, crucially, in my view, a whole lot less macho than the traditional format whereby some middle-aged geezer holds court, auteur-like.

Contemporary Coach Education across sports is embedded around the idea that the athlete/player/boy/

girl/star/novice is there to be supported, respected, emboldened. Coaches facilitate and prompt but most emphatically now they are expected to gift **ownership** of the pathway **to the player.**

This is a massive change and one which challenges coaches. Are we really generous enough? Can we shut up, bit more and just listen? Can we adjust the level of drive/graft/ambition, if necessary, to suit how the players *actually are?* Are we big enough to ask 'who is this for' often enough?

*

I rate this shift: don't see it as a downshift towards political correctness or softiedom or a step away from performance-level activity. We all know that performance-level sport will demand guts, hard graft and powerful discipline. We all know that at some stage the coach is gonna insist that such-and-such a technique/ movement/decision is 'essential'. But by this stage the athlete should be equipped (partly by excellent coaching) to make smart choices. Thus at the apex of player-centredness we have a kind of (hopefully) inviolable individual ownership of process, in which the (relatively invisible) coach has a not insignificant share.

*

My earlier example of Sports Science was of stat-engineered crib-sheets being held up, to shore up the performances of an IPL cricket franchise – or that might be the view of the purist. Batsmen being given signals to respond to, by their coaching teams. Live, in-play analysis from one or more 'stat-man', suggesting targets or responses to conditions/bowlers/states of the game. Pret-ty extraordinary stuff, right now, but likely to become standard, unless legislated against.[11]

Statistical analysis is only one tiny slither of the Sports Science sector, which stretches across psychology, physiology, injury/re-hab and injury-avoidance (AKA physical health) as well as technical, measurable conditioning and performance and way beyond. Let's just say it's a growth sector. What interests me here is the increased profile and relevance of much of this category, vast as it is and also the possible conflicts or contraflows I see developing.

How, for example does the rise of the Stat sit alongside the pre-eminence of the self-contained, confident player? Clearly it is entirely possible for **hot information** to merely 'arm' Player A, for her impending powerplay challenge. Yet is it also theoretically unhelpful for the same player and/or team-mates to fall into some level of reliance upon 'whatever's on the boards?'

*

How much should Statman get listened to? What, actually, are killer stats and what is white noise? When the great contemporary coaching cliché is 'trust the process', what does trust mean, now? Who decides and

---

[11] Not saying it should be, necessarily but do wonder how this might be regulated, down the line?

how are those decisions made, in the era of Just One Other Thing I Might Show You, Coach?

(Not at all making an argument against the use of stats; that argument is history, is lost. Repeat. Cricket, football, rugby, all are implanting analysis deeply, at the higher levels).

Plainly Young Guns are more likely to invest in stuff that still feels Fresh Outta Uni, than players and coaches of a particular age. (Mine). I imagine certain strong-willed pack leaders being resistant or even hostile to the juvenile boffins proffering their screens. But they have had to concede: welcome or otherwise stats now inform much of what competitive sporting strategy is about. Used with skill and discretion, they can richly inform performance. Marginal Gains for real.

*

It's inevitable that selection – to return to that one example – is and will be much influenced by information newly revealed. Within the layers of data thrust before him/her, the coach must decide what has value and where the new techno-richnesses are superfluous, indulgent or even misleading. Who has the skill, understanding and guts to make great calls about strategy and worth, live, in the moment, with 160 required, off 97 balls? Top, top coaches do that. I kinda hope that their instincts, their sense of the game, their twitching, irreducibly human antennae will always trump, somewhat, the Undeniable Message from the Screen. But yup, that's the romantic in me.

SIX – HOTEL BAGGAGE.

Julian Cope.[12] Hope he won't mind me saying that once upon a time, we were thrown together, for a briefish period. He was touring his 'World Shut Your Mouth' album; I was the barman at a certain West Walian hotel. One of the band members was an old mate who had somehow persuaded the management – such as it was – to stick an extra (Irish) gig on the end of the tour, in order to justify a Fishguard sailing and a mad weekend with us, in Pembs. (It turned out to be all-time-classic-level mad).

*

To give a flavour of the general proceedings, let me say that Copey at this time was drinking only pints of iced water (but still remained remarkably and endlessly perky) whilst flouncing abart the hotel in a grey woollen blanket and not much else. Day and night. Meanwhile, I was hosting the most incredible World Series of a tequila-slammer-drinking session in history, in the homely wee bar, with remaining band members and their two (I think) roadies.

---

[12] Again, shame on you if you're unfamiliar. Post-punk pop-rocker/ soft archaeologist and quite possibly English National Treasure (on Drugs). Great Moments include 'Treason' and 'Reward'.

It was magnificent, entertaining, prolonged havoc. Memories focus – if that's the word - around a spookily efficient production line of slammers being readied by yours truly, before being sealed by the left hand and thwacked onto a bar-top towel by the right, thus exploding the tequila and dry ginger in the glass into a glorious, ebullient pop-anthem of a drink. (Monstrous, if slammed expertly; try it. Joyful, effervescent, brain-bending. Don't do more than about – oooh, slix or sleven).

Our final, climactic sesh peaked with a spectacularly well-timed - that is, mid-slam - dropping of lower kit from one of the roadies, queueing with faux innocence at the bar. It will always be piteously childish (granted) but remains one of the funniest, most immaculately executed comedy routines I have ever witnessed. Only about six people were there to bear witness but the sight of that bare arse pogoing around our bar, post the consummate, triumphant necking of a humdingsnorter of a slammer, will (I hope) accompany me to the grave. We fell about.

There was payback but – wouldn't ya know it? - not to the King of Slapstick. Instead it was Adie, the Road Manager who later staggered up and out to the driveway for some cliff-top air. If he'd have strayed too far – it was the dead of a winter's night – he might have come a major cropper, with the beach about 150 feet below. But no. Adie thinks a little exercise might be mildly diverting: grabs hold of an *extremely small* bike, belonging to the infant child of the proprietors and proceeds to gambol around the gravel drive.

In truth this is mostly assumption. Nobody saw it but the evidence – gravel, *embedded*, deeply, into his face and palms – spoke for the adventure when he returned, like some stricken ghost, to the bar. Our horror at the sight was matched by the prospect of getting the poor bloke to hospital, sharpish. We were all blootered: don't tell my mum or the authorities that the barman took the helm.

When we arrived at Withybush Hospital after that 3 a.m. slalom, the victim slung between two of us as though crucified, the figure 'welcoming us in' was a distinctly unimpressed Hattie Jacques lookalike. (Important: this is I hope, neither sexist nor derogatory. Merely factual. The nurse/sister genuinely had the stature and the look of the indomitable star of those admittedly ethically dodgy films).[13]

Firstly, she assumed we'd been fighting; (I think it was a Saturday Night). Then, when she was sprayed just a little by that voice – Adie's, slurred and bubbling disturbingly with blood – the matron thought to sling us straight back out. Understandably. We did look like something out of a markedly vengeful saloon brawl.

Partly, I confess, the lady's ire had been raised because all three of us had absolutely fallen about at **what was said.** We really weren't trying to be rude, ungrateful or even unhelpful but we were drunk. And somehow, in a

---

[13] For you young 'uns – the 'Carry On' films. Hattie Jacques – often in matronly and/or notably voluptuous mode – starred.

moment of recognition, wit, madness, mischief and utter truth, Adie had offered the immortal words "A fellaff mebike." And we pretty much rolled round the walls. Still do.

*

We were saved only by a young guy, wandering past. We recognised each other from evenings at 'The Dru' and shared a laugh about the evident carnage. It was only as he began to fight his way into a white overall-coat-thing that I realised he was the doctor, clocking on. Us two sidekicks weren't allowed in, as he gently cleaned up and stitched up our compadre. However I do re-call trying to clamber high enough to *peer in*, through the glass section above the treatment-room's door. The same matron dismissed that possibility rather brusquely, I seem to recall.

*

But... *why is all this in here?!?* Let's list the ways.

- Goodish story, fair play – and true, every word.
- Dangerously challenging around that HJ issue. Should I simply not have mentioned it? Even though at the time, Jacques was a star... and there was an obvious lookalike thing going on? Might have been wiser but...
- *But mainly*: subsequently, with Adie not in any kind of shape, the band asked ME if I would go to Dublin with them as (temporary) Road Manager.

- *If I had done this,* **I don't think I'd be in the trade I'm now in** – *sports coaching* – because a) I might be dead b) I would probably have had a career in rock 'n roll - genuinely think this, either as a songwriter/guitar-player or in production/touring. It would have been life-changing, in terms of What I Do. And I love that **these things happen – or don't.**

- More abstractly but also more specifically/ personally Copesian, there is this: because of something Julian Cope sings, admittedly originally in the Teardop Explodes incarnation, in the New Age-tastic Anthem 'Treason', I think I am me.

- In one of the great, mad-delicious ironies, (well, one of mine), I'm not sure I can tell you exactly *what that something is* – and it's certainly not the only musical thing that makes me me – but this is one of the most fabulous and mysterious songs in the Thinking Person's Post-Punk Archive we're talking about. It melts into you; carries you somewhere. I got carried; blinking, innocently.

- Finally/ultimately… isn't everything musical? Maybe particularly the things we don't quite understand?

*

JC was a wildly eccentric talent – still is – with something of the Peter Pan/artsy odd-bod about him; something innocent, something on the edge of the endearingly profound and the daft. The whole idea of the song seems to be about truth, about what is real and therefore maybe precious: something about this lands with me every time.

As always the words aren't everything; it's in the swagger and swirl and chord-changes. But the refrain "UNTIL YOU REALISE... IT'S JUST A STORY" has always felt like a wonderful, abstract gathering-point, to me. It *could* say something about romance and the essence of things being indescribable. And it maybe offers some sort of license... to trust yourself? (I'm trying not to over-think this) but songs can be incredibly important, yes?

SEVEN - WHO WE ARE & THE MIGHTY VIC.

Because I'm frivolous and absolutely a Twitter fiend, I have been known to sling the odd hashtag around the place. I tend to do it ironically, despite realising how rarely irony works, on twitter: in fact in my experience, it can get you into bother.

I like the hashtag #lifesrichwotnots. It's never going to **trend,** of course but this is one of the reasons I use it. I like that the apostrophe can't be there and that it hints at quirky abstraction but also truth. That amongst the mess there is wonderful, profound stuff. 'Cos there is.

*

Just been binge-watching 'We Are Who We Are", on BBC-iplayer. It's a pop, 'modern', outrageous, brilliant, radical, freaky, intoxicated look at youth, sex, identity, set on an American military base in Northern Italy. It will offend conservatives and challenge liberals.

I'm still wondering (at the time of writing, obvs) if it's extraordinary in a gobsmackingly outstanding way or if the pile-up of *issues* is going to do my head in.[14] But whatever: there's one episode where teenage Fraser throws away a couple of lines 'on transgender' which do that impossible-wonderful thing whereby apparently weird, disposable telly explodes into really meaningful popular art. If you're *down wiv da kids* like me, you'll know it as **genius**. And it is. Go find it. Series 1, Episode 3. Around 13-14 minutes in – but do watch the whole series.

Fraser: 'We were told for ages that we were either males or females, okay? And that was that. Males would do certain things and females would do certain things – end of story. Transgender means... that you can cut that bullshit and instead you say "you know what? It's not that simple – it's not even binary."

It's a slam-dunk truth. It informs us. Let it do that.

*

Meanwhile, in another universe, running parallel, in 1930's-style football boots, (two sizes too small, as was the way), enter The Mighty Vic... and my bro's.

My youngest brother – there are four of us – is the fourth son of a fourth son. This always struck me as pretty cool, although cool is not a word I use, because 'American' and therefore faux – not of us. We were brought up in what is an undeniably fairly posh village, outside Grimsby. Parents both teachers, grand-parents

---

[14] Won't be for everybody but still strongly recommend.

pro' footballers and mill-workers or shopworkers, so we certainly wouldn't think of ourselves as Middle Class then, but our Mum and Dad climbed thataway, through honest hard work, both finishing up as headteachers.

Dad died cruelly young, at 44, of a massive cardiac arrest but Mum continued to graft away, leading two of the more challenging Primary Schools in Grimsby. Shortly before my father passed they bought a biggish semi: that house maybe re-positioned us but being of The North, I think we always felt that class was more a matter of how posh you *sounded*. We didn't sound posh, then - and I'm not sure we were 'comfortable' - until maybe that day some time after the tragedy that blighted our lives, when the insurance bloke called with a case containing £2,000. A day so weird that I'm not even sure if it happened.

*

I have an evolving relationship with age, feeling defiantly younger than the stats but looking suddenly oldish. And I get that it's *really embarrassing* when folks talk about the old days "when all we really had was a football". Well, sorry but this was our truth. The British Legion field, thirty yards away, big and generally blasted by gales from the North Sea, and The Park, three hundred yards down Fords Avenue, were our daily calling. There was cricket humming away on The Legion in the summer but we lived for football; hours and hours and hours of it. Change ends after five, ten goals; 'backs and forwards'. Lots of good little players, left 'alone', by loving and unconcerned parents day after day. It was simple: it was *of its time*. The levels of freedom and of dedication to the game are completely unthinkable now.

Grandpa played for United[15] Reserves but injury did for his career, early. Dad was a ver-ry solid player and we lads acquitted ourselves half-decently. In short it was a crazy-idyllic but inevitably kinda macho upbringing. Four lads and their mates: football in the blood.

I came to respect my Grandpa as a sporting hero only late-ish in my life – certainly after his death. Prior to that I loved him outside of all that relatively public stuff, for his implacable humour, his easy wit and a remarkable but quiet integrity. He epitomised something, maybe something generational and certainly something that sounds corny, about the power of common decency. The Mighty Vic (as I now call him) was a tremendous sportsman but also a pianist, a 'card' *and* a supremely modest fella. There was – like my Dad, like many Great Northern Men - absolutely **no side** to him. They understood the universe as a kind of expression of simple honesty, to which they manfully contributed, seeking nothing. This above all else is why they remain unimpeachably my idols.[16]

---

[15] Football People will know that this means Manchester United...

[16] Maybe remember this sentence when you finish the chapter. Please.

We Walton lads – generally two or three of us, anyway – got the train into Grimsby to watch the mighty Mariners play many times. Vic rarely came, despite having been a former player at the club. (To this day, I don't really know why... but find that absence interesting).

On one occasion I remember him coming with us and standing alongside me: this would be maybe about 1975. He watched and didn't say much. Pointed a bit. Town won and a sharp young winger called Tony Ford had been prominent. As we turned away at the whistle to trudge back to his car, Grandpa said this:

"He looks a good player, that darkie lad."

The Mighty Vic had said this without any edge, or malice. In fact possibly the reverse. He had liked what he'd seen of Town's new, flying winger. His remarks were made with a genuinely appreciative, low-key, Football Man's relish. Except of course that however commonplace that d-word might have been, at that time and however inoffensively meant – and I do stress it felt inoffensively meant – it was an appalling clanger. The fact that it was the mid-seventies and that he was probably seventy himself offers no excuse – merely context.

Vic was particularly well-placed to make an informed judgement about this young, black footballer *as a player*. But lost elsewhere. I am conflicted (to some degree) about where my Grandpa's 'innocence' in this matter begins and ends. It feels slippery, because of the lack of spite and maybe because I'm not best-placed to judge. Where you place it on the scale of casual racism to outright evil may not matter. Ultimately, he was wrong and the memory hurts.

EIGHT - JASPRIT BUMRAH: "IT'S GOT TO FEEL LIKE YOU".

Know this doesn't really work in the Real Writing World where it takes months or even years to get things into print but as I chirp away now, on Draft Numero Uno, Jasprit Bumrah[17] is (I trust) preparing to bed down with some satisfaction, after tearing into the Australians, in Melbourne. (Boxing Day Test, 2020. He took a very fine four-fer as the home side subsided to 195 all out).

Bumrah is This Year's Demi-god, for connoisseurs of swiftish bowling. People love something about him; he is special – and especially effective - without necessarily looking *that likely*. He is a decent specimen, as opposed to a giant (like Starc), or a fabulous athlete (like Archer). Bumrah has goodish pace – towards 140 clicks, typically – but arguably not quite that searing bullet-thing that the really express guys have: or possibly more accurately, that's not, it seems, *his most significant weapon.* He seems, somehow, a lovely, undemonstrative bloke. So how come this extravagant drama all around him?

Like Anderson, perhaps, the fella has 'skills'.

---

[17] Indian fast bowler, known for quality and for his quirky action.

It may be a mistake to try to capture what it is that Bumrah has, either via stats – though of course there will be some value, here – or, yaknow, through mere words, but let's measure out our run and have a thrash at it. Part of the fun, yes?

Bumrah's action is pleasingly un-pleasing. It's relatively idiosyncratic and therefore distinctive, in a world where it feels like bowlers may be being over-coached and roboticised. It's possibly easier to describe what it's not, than what it is.

It is not classical; not even fluent, particularly. It's not Anderson, Ishant, Cummins, or anybody else. The run-up is short and features something of a leftward-leaning phase, an odd cradling of the arms and a relative absence of threat or dynamism, until the last possible moment. Then at least one spare arm appears, to fling hands wantonly high before that final spearing, discombobulating wheel. Delivery is utterly legal... but almost offensive, in aesthetic terms. Except that because it's so patently his own, we love it – we love *him*. Bumrah is dismissing the received wisdoms of the universe and flicking those vees alongside Buttler. He's doing those things *for us*.

But how come he's so effective, so respected (apart from that refreshing quirkiness?)

My instinct is that he bowls a killer length ver-ry often, as well as producing outstanding, menacing deliveries. I'm honestly not clear if this means batsmen are rather worn-down by his bowling - *undermined,* by a series of challenges - as opposed to being undone by individual pearlers, or not. (I do recognize that all bowling registers itself in *spells* – love the word, love the concept – but is it possible that some bowlers weaponize a kind of cumulative efficacy or brilliance more than others? And wow; could we ask a stat-man to confirm that?)

If Bumrah has a killer ball, it's probably his yorker. (For non-cricketers, this is a ball that hurtles directly for the batter's toes, or the base of the stumps. There is no bounce to contend with... until it's too late). Bumrah has an in-swinging yorker that seems to gather pace and momentum as it scorches towards that flummoxing gap *underneath* the bat. It's a jewel of the international game – of any game.

A further thought: an impenetrably hunch-tastic one. There is something about the way Bumrah's non-bowling arm follows through, incredibly fully and extravagantly and maybe threateningly(?), that may be wonderfully central to the fella's bewitching of batsmen. (In fact this may even relate to both arms: the resulting impression being like an unfurling of secretly-coiled limbs – extra arms, even). Normal mortals - like yaknow, me - either struggle or simply cannot or could not ever 'finish' the delivery with that degree of flourish. I seriously wonder if that specific, extravagant windmilling of his is somehow a part of the enchantment.

I do a little research – yes really! – and find something interesting. Shoaib Akhtar,[18] a.k.a. 'The Rawalpindi Express', interviewed on t'internet, has spoken of how

---

[18] Former opening bowler, Pakistan. Electrifyingly quick.

Bumrah is 'smart', in part because of how he uses the wind. Shoaib accepts that the combination of subtle changes in length within a supremely consistent 'corridor' are inevitably major but also notes how his own predecessors from Pakistan, Wasim and Waqar would check out wind speeds and direction in the belief that they could just draw an edge – literally, sometimes – by making tiny shifts in pace and/or alignment around the crease. He sees Bumrah operating with the same cuteness, adding just enough variety around a challenging, metronomic line to unpick the batsman, wind-assisted, or otherwise.

So there is a sort of general acceptance in the game that Bumrah is a craftsman, a talent, that he is exceptional and that somehow all of us get a minor share in his success, because he's 'breaking the mould', just a little. That weird shuffle and arm-sling combo might, on another day, belong to Youngie, from the Thirds. That not entirely convincingly A-list physique feels reassuringly familiar. And yet... look at him now: bowling like a god!

Shoaib Akhtar, astonishingly, bowled at least two deliveries that were clocked beyond 100 m.p.h. Bumrah, like most opening bowlers, sets it down there at around 85 – sometimes plus. Quick enough. But for him to bowl even that swiftly is pretty extraordinary, given his approach. Archer does something of a low-kneed, low-key shuffle in, but he at least has an athlete's form and grace, plus a fluent, whip-lasher of an arm. It's harder to immediately see or imagine where Bumrah generates his gas from.

Bowling coaches - I'm thinking here of Steffan Jones and Ian Pont, both of whom produce striking technical and other material on pace - accept that a certain portion of bowling speed comes from running in hard and efficiently. Ineluctable, surely? And the simplest way to increase bowling speed is to run in faster. None of this equates to long, quick run-ups being The Key, of course; they just sometimes work, or *contribute*. Breathtakingly so, in the case of say, Michael Holding.

Bumrah is again an outlier, here, but (*because all things are complex, yes?*) I wonder if the brevity of his run-up could be a factor in the level of threat he offers. That amble/stutter/breakout – can it really only be seven steps? – represents maybe five seconds of approach (so less than many other quicks), in which the batter must gather and set, before the trigger, the movements, as the bowler hits the crease. It's possible that this *different rhythm* and the whole staccato whirligig thing that is the Bumrah action is a little disconcerting to face. Does the whole Bumrah Experience (as opposed to pure pace of delivery) somehow hurry, or subvert batsmen? Is *difference*, or how much is difference a part of the *effect*, here? Given that the guy can also pepper you with stuff that might swing, cut or bounce, it's surely tough to settle against this?

In no sense do I want to underappreciate Bumrah by overstating his 'uniqueness'. He's in the top handful of bowlers in the world and generally recognised as India's finest on merit, not because folks love his eccentricity. The variety of deliveries in his armoury, the deceptive, challenging length, the glorious yorkers and leg-cutters, all tick the Great Quick box. But is there not even more pleasure, richer entertainment to be had, given his unconventionality?

As a former bowler who now coaches, and specifically as someone who does harbour some concerns that any suggestion of a one-size-fits-all/heavily directed approach to the art is constricting and possibly spirit-crushing, I enjoy what Bumrah is. My hunch (from long experience, from loving how bowling feels) has always been that however much technical or theoretical analysis might suggest that *particular ways* are effective, or advised, individual comfort, individual movements – rather than idealized – support bowlers better. I have been known to offer the following, to bowlers who may be wondering whether they need to be 'tweaking something', to gain pace or advantage.

Bottom line? It's got to feel like you.

I stand by that.

NINE - OPINION.

Some of you will know I'm a political animal: I've been ver-ry torn as to whether to unleash on that here. In short, though I feel both entitled to and in some ways inclined, I'm going to hold that stuff back – or most of it.

Goddammitt that feels cowardly, shallow and unworthy, given that I can make a pret-ty decent argument that any discourse of any depth has to accept context. And in our (British/Western?) case, let's face it, the political matrix is poisonously relevant and contributes heavily to all our divisions and arguably all our decisions.

Hang on. Does politics intrude into how I/we/you select our cricket teams? Probably not – or minimally. But does politics intrude into how we select our *wider* teams... or make other decisions of import? Hell, yes! Decisions spring from opinion and attitude as much as they do from facts.

*

Here's the deal: I'll step away from party politics and away from Campaigning Mode – go to @bowlingatvinny[19]

---

[19] My less-used but more vocal twitter feed, where lurketh the anger and artsy-ness I try to exclude from @cricketmanwales. Gateway to bowlingatvincent.com

for some of that if you wish – in return for a brief, broad sweep at something.

Current events continue to brutally remind us that racism is everywhere and that many of us White Folks are either outright guilty of it, carry related baggage, or wish we could escape from our White Guilt more completely. (Go read Saad/Eddo Lodge/Olusoga/Hirsch. I just did: it was fabulous and enriching and truly educational).[20] Prejudice is real… and crippling… and multi-layered. We need to take a look at ourselves.

*

So, *broadly,* what motivates our responses, our feelings – the decisions we take? How *innocent* of bias or bigotry or compound complexity can they be? How 'pure?' I'm fascinated and maybe haunted a tad, by this. It's opaque, mysterious territory, but I do know that we have to – in the words of Black activism – check on our privileges. That means contemplation of the more excoriating kind.

I increasingly think that this needs to be a part of what it means to be a decent citizen and yes, I have concerns about our level of citizenship. Oh, and though I understand that (for example) the #BlackLivesMatter movement is about **levels of urgency** and therefore absolutely rightly has a kind of precedency, my concerns/interests/questions are not just about race.

---

[20] Mean this. White guys like me need to listen.

Let's play a game where we all think of times – or maybe just one time - where we may have gotten things badly wrong. Maybe publicly, though not necessarily. Something that has that added torque of being somewhere along the scale of prejudice, or has that possibility. So you are not just reflective or quizzical on this; you feel like you may have humiliated yourself or leaked a bit of the baggage that may lurk within that otherwise decent soul.

I'll go first – obviously.

*

I wrote about Amy Winehouse,[21] shortly after her death, trying to grapple with "honest feelings" about her talent, her death, her voice. I was ver-ry conscious that my concern about her voice being more a projection than a real *instrument of hers* cut across both the grain of the moment – that is, her overdose – and popular feeling about her genius. It's not simple but *then*, I simply felt (personally) unable to trust in that voice, on those records.

I am now clear that Winehouse really was special and am less concerned about whether she 'jazzed-up' her voice. So was I outright wrong, back then? Was I shielding deep resentments against heavy drug-users, or what? (On reflection – yes, probably. But in case you're wondering, I really am very clear that anti-semitism was

---

[21] Extraordinary singer-songwriter. Brought down by drugs. I under-estimated her achievement.

not a factor. Really clear). However sure I might be that I was just trying to be honest about that voice... *what was really in play?* Poor taste? Misogyny? If I can write two arguably deeply problematic blogs about Amy Winehouse what the hell can I trust myself with?

*

If you're looking for an explanation about what this means/why this is in the book then a) don't but b) maybe consider this another personal investigation into that whole baggage/truth/motive scene, or c) put it down to indulgence. But wow. Just me? How opinions are formed, informed, or the opposite. Am I wrong to think that it's healthy to pick over this? Is this not rich territory? Rich but scary but necessary?

In conclusion, let me bring out the B-word. Brexit. Let me challenge you, sagacious reader by saying I think that whole malarkey was an obvious function of racism. Small-mindedness. Folks conflating 'immigration' with 'our own rights'; seeking to blame, seeking an outlet for their prejudice.[22] For me, appalling – for you, maybe something different. But can we agree that it may be the single most divisive event in our lives?

*

Here's the thing. How do we then work together, function together, when it seems so hard to relate? How

---

[22] This – this book, actually - is as much a confession as an allegation. So yup, *ironies*...

do I accept (what feel like) your morally reprehensible views, and move on? How do you stop yourself from bawling out the pinkos?

I think the answer for me personally may be to put myself back in those school or club changing-rooms. To picture those guys who farted and giggled and bore their obligations to political correctness (hah!) lightly. And yet they were the best, funniest mates I ever had. They fizzed with a kind of real, earthbound genius that was in some sense truer than any philosophical calling. They had flaws: they had value. In fact they *made me* because their brilliance, loyalty and (mostly) working class honesty both empowered me and made any level of ease with privilege and snobbery elsewhere im-bloody-possible. So I honour them and am genuinely, humbly grateful for that revelation, which I hold with me always.

Hah, once more there's a counterpunch – inevitably, things are complex, right?

Weirdly, maybe offensively, it feels like part of our togetherness, which I am clear went right past 'bonding' into authentic Brotherhood, was that we acted like Neanderthals, half the time. Reconcile that? I do and have, partly because I remember virtually no substantive prejudice, from back then. Kev Peel, Pete Emson, Col Humphries, Steve Bramley, Gaz Sanderson – you're still my heroes now.

TEN – UNWEIGHTING.

Trawling through my back catalogue is absolutely not what I set out to do, here but forgive me a nostalgia trip. Cricket People may be reassured, possibly, to hear that it is very specifically about things that may be uniquely cricketty. The very first blog wot I wrote, over on bowlingatvincent.com, in response to something surprisingly (counter-intuitively?) intelligent from Aussie bigmouth Ian Chappell.[23] From 2011, when my own relatively occasional bullishness apparently matched that of the former Baggy Green monster.

Am inserting the whole bloody lot a) for the word count and b) because this is history, right here. And c) it's actually medium-interesting... and almost relevant to the discussion we're nearly having; you know, the one about **readiness.** Am guessing Wimbledon must have just been on. But it's cricket. Haven't changed a word.

*

'Unweighting'. From bowlingatvincent.com, June 24th, 2011.

---

[23] Chappell – or 'Chappelli' – captained Australia in the seventies. Notably bullish. Clashed with opposition, clashed with administrators: famously clashed with Ian Botham.

Hey look there's no point in pretending life/business/ relationships/quality of backhand are islands of independence from each other; no point. On the contrary, as I am about to prove, even if your nature is to quietly shriek pallid protest against activity in all its wondrous forms – ya *wuss* - you cannot deny the power of sport and the need to be ready.

Preparation? Everywhere. Man in sport there's a *spooky* amount, an industry - an absolutely sexsational amount of 'ready positions' like, for starters. Tennis the currently obvious one; receiver with knees bent, weight slightly forward, hands in front, gusset slightly exposed. Rugby (backs); hands out in front, attracting the ball, offering a target, inviting that moment of caress, of possession.

The talk in coaching is deliciously loaded with this stuff. And the transferability of these sopping metaphors is meaning frankly Frankie, you ain't got no escape; not in the office, not in 'sales', not in bed, much less out-on-the-park. And yet, amongst the daft-punk dribbles, the cod-psychology... there's some really byoodifull stuff man.

Take fast bowling. It's an admittedly staccato dance that grippingly, thrillingly transcends its technically-heavy brief. (Sheesh - did I nick that from Ronay?) Whatever, lately think Anderson 'when it's coming out nicely'. Jimmy aka The Burnley Express – in his pomp, does deal in majestic simplicities; purring in, expressing repeatedly creamy smooth bursts; simples.

Simples but superceded surely, by the intoxicating
Michael Holding at his peak, 'pace' being then at that
perfect moment where something beyond words was,
really, momentarily described. And during that
alarmingly fluent Caribbean blur, amidst the ecstatic
barrage from Marshall, Walsh, Garner et al, we strain
for ... sentences like that last one... where words
transparently fail. Or maybe we simply concede,
smiling, and not a little awestruck, (that) that was
bloody *unplayable*.

And now we find ourselves marking out the run-up to
some truth; particularly if we think of the batter.

Take my word for it here that when you face fast
bowling you are shitting your pants. No question. For
maybe only a few minutes, but parping like a good 'un,
nonetheless. So, with apologies to Jessica Oosit Parker
in "Sex and The City" mode, if, say Michael Holding is
that challenging, *that* much of an extreme test; *how do
you get ready for that?*

Unweighting. Ian Chappell - yes! Aussie skipper and
general arse.

Extraordinarily (and, sharing a birthday with
I.T.Botham, I ask no forgiveness for the implied anti-
antipodeanism here) Ian Chappell formulated the
following really rather beautiful and insightful concept.

Simply put, unweighting is a process necessary for a
batsman to enable 'survival' against quick bowling. So
this usually happens most – and most obviously – at the

beginning of an innings, or when the dreaded or lusted after new ball is taken. (See what I mean? Sopping). Pre-delivery or 'trigger' movements occur in the batsman, either consciously or not, in order to facilitate, to cope, to avoid getting hurt or out. Because the ball may come down fucking hard and fast. Batters may open their eyes wider/crouch intently whilst setting their neck/flex their knees/give up and dollop one.

Generally coaches identify two movements of the bat before hitting the ball, at that crucial heart-thumping moment when (godforbid), Holding is unleashing. There is bat-lift and then bat-swing; the former involving simply raising the bat from the ground, the latter the judgement and immediate subsequent execution of how much or little you're going to swing the bat. The minutiae of both can naturally – and I use the word advisedly - vary from player to player but Chappell's view has been that these ripples of the wrist or micro-steps or other habitual or rehearsed or coached movements are key. Likewise the momentum or freedom engendered by the transfer of weight from one foot to another. Unweighting.

Thus, sagacious reader, the batter's ready position against extreme pace has to be an exquisitely timed and balanced and consistent and fluent and enabling stance for that which may be unplayable. So can you move instantly (in a balanced etc. etc. way) forward or back? Can you withdraw from the stroke? Can you duck? Can you look in control and not give the bowler and the infield signs of encouragement? Are you, in these milliseconds, rhythmical and composed and *absolutely at the top of your game?* Man it's a wonderful, frightening test.

And how do we transfer its richness, its poetry and its latent dynamism to work... to life... to relations(hips)... to bed?!?

Can you find it, this unweighted state? Are you ready? Are you?

*

Hey of course this is embarrassing. But I still think it captures something about facing fast bowling. About the hardness of the ball and the hyper-edginess of the moment.

Can't honestly remember why it turned so sexualised, at the end, there. Other than me having an ironic pop at dumb machismo – something you may be surprised to hear I've been doing since 1847 - and/or referring to "Sex In The City", which was massive and er, influential at the time of writing. Like both the word unweighting and the impression of flow and release and poetry, even, around it. Still incredulous that a concept so lovely and demonstrably civilized came out of the fella Chappell. But, to re-cap, readiness is all.

INTER-CHAPTER TWO – METAPHORS.

My crazy-mixed metaphors and general, diabolical liberty-taking annoy some people. I get that. My excuse or explanation can only be something about expression and urgency and trying to truthfully capture the swirl of the world. So however unkempt it might feel, let me put before you the notion that this free-wheeling absurdism[24] is driven by the blameless urge to *record,* to make honest social documents. Hilariously, I'm actually working pretty hard at it.

Fully understand that some folks will dislike the indulgence but I can't for now, get past the autobiographical and the felt: these are things I know. My need to inhabit that ground could be either from insecurity or ambition: your call. The writing might be endearing or embarrassing: your call. Clap in the street, or don't.

*

---

[24] Got called this by a dramaturg back in 1846. Possibly over a play called "My Kaleidoscope Says... The World Gets Better Every Day". Fact! Wanted to put Free-wheeling Absurdist in the employment descriptor of my passport, for years.

I support and am drawn to artists – what they do, what they say - because the overwhelming majority are trying to find profound answers to profound questions in a way that probably nobody else is. They ask about the meaning of life, because they don't know what else to do; because they feel it's their job, or calling. And most just quietly get on with it.

Easy to be cynical about that stuff but that level of integrity is precious: you hold up your flag.

In this book leg-spin might be carpentry and batting might be business. Coaching might be about reading the human, as much as it's about structure or instruction. Experience, sights, sounds; everything feeds in to the search for understanding. To almost quote my mate Ted Lasso[25] - *that's part of the fun.*

---

[25] Wantonly generous-spirited American 'soccer' coach imported to rescue Richmond AFC, ailing Premiership club, in affecting Apple TV drama. The daft bugger thinks that making people better is more important than winning matches...

ELEVEN – BAD STUFF IN THE GAME(S).

O-kaay, maybe we need to lighten up. And what better way than to talk about things that *really 'get us going?'* I'll go first, off the top of my head: boom!

- Minor one – so this is not in order – personalised tracksuits/kit etc. What's all that about, really? Just arrogance?

- Media Training. Of anybody, pretty much. Designed to suck the life and soul out of everything.

- Corporate thinking. (Know we've suddenly gone ver-ry broad but... surely you don't have to be anti-capitalist to call out the dumbness at the heart of corporate thinking?) Make the shallow feel sexy. Invent a language and shield inside it. 'Channel' things. Make sales. Make this an angry club.

- Mourinho. And possibly Harry Kane.

- Dishonesty and cynicism more generally, in sport. Our great escape traduced.

Your go in a minute but... let's start with those last two.

Mourinho.[26] The guy's poisonous. That bleak, Trumpian narcissism, those endless 'mind games'. God what a bore, he is. What a dead soul. Experienced enough to hold a top club in contention but so deeply miserable a spirit that you just know his darkness will drive his players from him soon enough. The fact that he got the Spurs job after his relatively mediocre and often unsavoury work over the last few years speaks volumes about the state of the football universe. It's crass; it's delusional; it lacks values as well as value.

More than that it lacks judgement in nearly every sense. Mourinho has for two or three years been widely viewed as a spent or deteriorating force. Players are at least as likely to hate his vanity and his late-stage bus-parking as they were once queueing to sign for him. But he gets Big Projects because the whole of creation – well, impressionable chairmen – get sucked in. We/they are attracted, apparently by the noise, the fuss, the column inches and/or the notion that he's a winner... because he *was*. We've been algorithmned again.

*

Spurs were top (November, 2020) but it didn't and couldn't last. What *will* last is the sense that despite having outstanding attacking players – Son, Kane, Bale, Moura – they opted for a deeply negative mindset

---

[26] As I write *this*, manager at Tottenham Hotspurs FC. Still being relatively successful - or not? (Discuss). Still being undeniably excruciatingly negative... and dolefully 'closed'.

whenever the bigger games came round. Or let's be plain; Mourinho dictated so. He may not be alone in this but no wonder he failed so utterly to galvanise the enigmatic but ravishingly gifted Bale.

*

Those of us who picture Tottingham as a home for cosmopolitan flash and dash and skill – think on the **football contributions** of Venables, Hoddle, Redknapp, Villa, Ardiles, Gascoigne, Sheringham, Erikson for example – have been swiftish perhaps but unapologetic in shunting Spurs towards the Team We All Love To Hate column. And that's been Mourinho: he breeds vituperation and discontent.

Imagine being a fabulous talent now and hearing that Jose wanted you? Imagine how quickly you'd be shrieking at your agent to phone Klopp or Pep. For his relentless suffocation of joy, his insulting and criminally miserablist Press Conferences and maybe particularly his blame-the-players schtick, Mourinho is top of my Bad Stuff in the Games pile.

*

Of late, his captain – England's captain – has been clawing his way up there, too. Harry Kane.

OK. Hands up; generational things are in play again, here. (But please remember that if I am authentic anything it is, or arguably was, football. It's a game I grew up through, a game I reckon I can still read).

*

Clearly many of us older guys and gals could write a book on the changes in football that we don't like. Simulation; the shift towards non-contact; VAR;[27] the concentration of power and resources. But I'm guessing one of the most irksome – no, outright rage-inducing - is the striker not seeking to strike. Kane is absolutely not alone in this.

Once upon a time, any of us who got a whiff of goal – say when the space opened up in front, allowing that glorious charge towards the keeper – would narrow our eyes, instinctively burst on and try to smash the ball into the top corner. Now the first thought is to draw a pen.

Know what? I don't mind sounding miserablist about this. Or judgmental. I see strikers running across centre-halves to draw a foul and a red. I see extra jinks in the box to *draw contact*.[28] I watch the obvious dives and the subtler dangling of the leg to claim a touch, an advantage. Usually this means a penalty but sometimes also the removal of an innocent opponent from the game – as a 'bonus'. This registers with some of us as sleaze, not sport.

---

[27] Video Assistant Referees. In theory to eliminate error from officials and ease the grief over controversial decisions. In practice – ludicrously, this surely could be made to work? – a nightmare.

[28] One of the central curses. Players now look to 'draw contact' in the expectation that officials (including VAR) might penalise the opposition. It's obvious, it's appalling and it's an insult to the game.

Unhelpfully, one response is anger. I suspect it doesn't further our case for the moral high-ground but part of me wishes Jackie Milburn[29] could publicly execute these people for crimes against the game: club them to death like seal-pups. (Or maybe not – 'cos seal-pups are innocent. But you get the unappealingly inflammatory drift). Yes; am fully aware that any anti-sleaze rage marks us 'moralists' out as dinosaurs and weirdos who should just 'get real'. But no.

No embarrassed backward steps. Why should the idea that one of the profound pleasures of sport - the comradeship which spreads *across teams*, out of respect - be Jurassic? Why should it be naïve to think that being honest is good and that therefore this can complement other substantive plusses, in sport? None of us are saying that being sporting is everything. We're saying that it feels important as part of the whole. It's good to watch, good to experience: players competing to the max knowing, at some level, that cheating or simulation transgresses a shared code.

*

What's the *source* of all this? Is it about culture? Has the mindlessness or lack of self-awareness of Top Top Players (which no doubt always existed), either sky-rocketed or merely raised its profile in the manner of the age? Is the ethical lacuna a sort of necessary parallel to the disturbing level of self-obsession in the general

---

[29] Former Newcastle and England centre-forward, now presumed gyrating in his grave.

population, especially the young, many of whom now *really do* blankly take dozens or even hundreds of auto-snaps of themselves *every day?* In the echoing chambers of the Instaworld, it's hard to make any relatable case for a moral dimension in sport. Decency ain't big, or trending, on Twitter and Tik Tok.

If the apparently unreflective Kane spoke about 'his responsibilities' they would be dispiritingly empty words. That *his fault?* Who or what is directing him and us, these days?

The universe has conspired to make even talk of role-modelling seem facile, when it should have/could have meaning. Something has eaten away at our ability to judge, think, concentrate, feel. Those things matter less than how many likes, how acceptable our look is, how far into the reassuring centre we can claw. Football Legends diving are just a high-profile equivalent of wider vacancies, shallower cultures. The dumb fuckers think they're doing their jobs.

*

In this respect, does football – the Premier League in particular - more accurately reflect society than any other sport? (Interestingly, the rugby community savages footballers, both for their physical feebleness and their lack of honour: there's another book in that!)

Is everything now, about notoriety, about **followers,** about *being visible but un-conscious?* And therefore diving simply a part of the vogue for 'making things happen' and/or *succeeding?*

Is #modernlife really that #rubbish? Plainly this part of it is.

Harry Kane has drawn attention recently because of the way he sidles underneath airborne defenders, in order to both gather fouls and put the possibility of serious injury into the mind of the guys marking him. He absolutely knows they may over-balance and fall heavily and out of control. It's dangerous and it really stinks. He might call it 'looking after myself' and some clown like Keown might call it clever. No. It's shit.

Postscripts.

Understand that there's a danger with any book – especially one as aspirationally urgent as this - that you can fall into a never-ending series of additions, between moment of 'finishing' and moment of publishing. Hope to avoid that: feel justified *enough* in inserting the following. Here: things have happened.

MOURINHO.

Jose Mourinho was sacked, by Tottenham Hostpur FC, on 20th April 2021. As I now write – the day after – there is a relative dearth of information/explanation from either the man himself or the club on this,[30] so I can merrily insert the label **performance-related** to the event, whilst seriously considering adding a cheesy-grin

---

[30] Initially, the club simply stated that Mourinho (and his **four support staff**) were 'relieved of their duties'.

emoji. Jose's Tottingham have got beat ten times in the season already. Unacceptable – so no more.

Fascinatingly, the eminent sportswriter Paul Hayward speculated on the Twitters as to the likelihood of Mourinho *actively engineering* his own demise, by yet more unnecessarily barbed bleating earlier in the week – again aimed at his own players' alleged inadequacies. A deliberate step too far?

Hayward is not alone in thinking that the man is perfectly capable of timing a particularly offensive moan so as to bundle his board into action. (Not entirely convinced, mind, by the argument made elsewhere that this is about skilfully tripping severance payments; my hunch being that despite being a cynical barsted, the Departed One a) doesn't need the money and b) weirdly, perhaps, may not be that driven by cash alone). Don't like the bloke but think he may simply be more intelligent than that. And yet... it might be remiss not to note to the universe that Jose the Jolly One may have received a total of upwards of 70 million smackeroos compensation following exits from his various clubs.

Yup. Reported as 77.5 million pounds on t'internet – which as we know, is gospel. Reminder: much of this money is for having *failed*. Mourinho chose to leave Leira (of Portugal), Porto - ditto, obvs - and Inter Milan. Elsewhere he has got what we might term the golden hoof.

Perhaps two of the more interesting facets of this story are the 'why *now*, precisely?' question, arising from the imminence of an EFL (or is it Carabao?) Cup Final versus Manchester City, and the minor rumblings about whether Mourinho could have done something uncharacteristically decent – namely flatly refused to countenance any personal involvement in a European Super League. That final was but five days after: the ill-fated ESL project was announced the day of the sacking. Interesting? Unknown territory, for now.

My final final word[31] on The Special One is that he is/was bad stuff in the game and I hope he does the decent thing and checks out, permanently. Go live. Stop being melancholically monstrous to journo's, players, everybody around. Word is there is a charming man in there somewhere. Read, cook, chill, entertain people but disappear from football.

(Fat chance).

THE EUROPEAN SUPER LEAGUE.

Wow. Can you even imagine the surge of renegade, pyro-maniac energy flashing around a particular psycho-purist's body over this baby? You're going to get off lightly – I am an inch away, I promise, from finding the nearest heavy-duty amphetamine supplier and staying up for eight days solid to burn through another blistering, socially-conscious sport/politics missive. You

---

[31] My final final update is that predictably Mourinho landed a job somewhere nice, somewhere BIGGISH, within a month. AS Roma. After entertaining the Talksport listeners, during the Euros, Jose heads back to Italy.

know I really could be the bloke to metaphorically immolate or disembowel Messrs Henry and co for their smooth, smiling, fascistic, evil-neo-liberal 'disruption' to our game. But this will be brief.

*For those who were either hiding behind the settee, in April 2021, or cruising round some wifi-less atoll, here's what was proposed. A new, additional European football competition for a bunch of allegedly elite clubs. Played midweek, theoretically a Big Noise and a big earner. Fans guffawed at the cheek of it then revolted. A) because the thing was a sealed unit – no promotion or relegation. B) because it would plainly drain money, glamour and interest away from the existing leagues and cups. C) because it was driven **only** by the club supremos, with **no discussion amongst players, managers, fans.** It really was a kind of coup.*

Whilst we need to avoid falling into some snake-pit of xenophobia here, it was clear that foreign ownership of clubs was central to the whole humiliating shitshow. Folks with obscene wedges of money wanting more: folks who probably don't even like the game, much less follow it, know it or love it.

*

They came, they shat on us, we retaliated - broke out our proper, big-league muck-spreaders. The Shameless Six,[32] (in Chris Sutton's words), concocted or were

---

[32] Six English clubs were amongst the potential Super Leaguers. Man Utd, Man City, Liverpool, Arsenal, Tottenham and Chelsea.

drawn into the biggest and most laughably unaware plan in the history of heisting and we absolutely slaughtered them. (Note: by 'we' here, I am shamelessly lumping myself in there with the heaving, outraged masses; the supporters; those who care; those who were/are absolutely right).

Within 72 hours of the Super League announcement, one of its chief proponents – J W Henry, *in charge* but also distantly connected to Liverpool FC – was apologising. Having no doubt coiffured the climbdown over several hours of intense rehearsal at Message Massage HQ, the American did a passable job of affecting a manner both responsive and essentially humane; like the leader of some faultlessly worthy green energy project, having accidentally crushed two badgers and an orchid en route to site. "We heard you", he said, with humble authority.

This apology - aimed, I'm guessing at the supporters of LFC as opposed to any pancaked mammals - falls stunningly short. It's both the right thing and a jarring, mind-bending fraud. The problem being that they (let's call them the Henrys) **chose** to **completely bypass us** *before*.

It may be that some of the Super Leaguers were sufficiently cretinous to fail to realise there would be an enormous, vitriolic backlash, but most chose to cruise past that notion, flicking the vees at lifelong supporters of their clubs. It was of the times in that it was a grotesque and blatant transgression against common decencies, commonly understood, and a monument to and for excess. More money. More 'growth'. More filthy, shiny, unnecessary product.

Typically, Twitter nailed it. Not just in terms of the expression of noisy, justifiable hoo-ha but also by intelligent reduction. It was there I saw Football People not just getting angry but unpicking the putrid essence of the Super League proposals. The whole thrust of this was to do with the production of new, saleable *content*. Not football; not competition, or sport, or excitement. Content. Produced by and for people who don't give a toss about this or any other game. For the benefit of the Henrys.

These dumb clowns really do just want a bigger market share; more billions; more yachts. How gratifying that inspired and overwhelming public dissent squished their sordid ambitions. How cruel that the uprising against rank avarice and corruption will probably end there. As will the UK government's concern for that which is owned by the hearts of the ordinary.

TWELVE – BATTING.

Cricket is not without its snobbery – did you notice? - and I don't just mean that Middle Class/Upper Class staging for much of the game. Like most things that people genuinely love and feel attachment towards, or ownership of, there is a strong sense of *how it should be played*. Hence the Spirit of Cricket.[33] (Friends, you may be relieved to hear I'm not going there!) No; I'm going briskly towards **orthodoxy.**

The dictionary says of orthodoxy that it is 'authorized or generally adopted theory, doctrine or practice'. Fair enough. This noun transfers across not unhelpfully to one of the adverbs/adjectives describing batting: orthodox batting. You could perhaps draw up a wider, richer cricketty subset which might include classical, expansive, doughty and in the modern era, boomtastic. Words which capture the how and very often the who, of the genre. Boycott might be doughty (or just dour) and Gower classical, maybe. Everybody in the contemporary short-format game is necessarily

---

[33] Lots of spicy discussion around about how cricket *should be* - what 'spirit' it should be played in. Fully understand how the traditional view might be read as a kind of ridicupomp: what right has cricket to view itself as morally/ethically superior? So light touch needed. (But) personally think it's fair enough to quietly aspire towards good sportsmanship and comradeship.

boomtastic. Suffice to say that it's not just afficionados of cricket that can picture what the words mean in terms of the players' *manner*: these things cross sports, inform wider vistas.

For what feels like millennia, batting coaches have preached orthodoxy, in the main. Earlier in this book I plucked the idea from the ether that it was about the year 2000 that things changed, in terms of coaches swivelling towards something more generous; something which supported the athlete's capacity to discover and execute in their own way. That date is largely spurious but **player-centrism** has featured a very real, concomitant and powerful surge towards 'positivity'.

*

In July 2019, Jason Roy, the South African born but England star of T20 and 50 over formats was selected to play Test Cricket for the first time, against Ireland, at Lords. It was a 'one-off Test', according to the BBC website. The selection panel had been Ed Smith, James Taylor and Trevor Bayliss, plus, as tradition would have it, the captain, Joe Root. It was a bold call.

There is context, including the opposition, who, with all due respect were and remain – much as I love 'em - Test minnows, meaning less risk of embarrassment for England players and selectors alike. *Theoretically*. But also there was the seemingly endless capacity for an apparently half-decent England Test Team to slump to 33 for 3 every time they turned out. (Again stats may not entirely bear this out; again the truth is maybe in how things felt). Root's side had foundations of clay. With Alastair Cook's retirement from international cricket in September 2018 and the lack of solid replacements (at that stage), Smith, Taylor and Bayliss had gambled. Or had they?

Roy was not an unorthodox player so much as a challenging fit for the Test game. His oeuvre was the relentlessly aggressive one. He had a swagger – or worse, or better – and a stunning eye. His role was typically to smash straight through the line of the (white) ball, on placid pitches and/or carve to all points of the compass. He was and is one the best in the world at this explosive opening gambit. But that's a *different game*. The ball is different in Tests.[34] The intensity and duration of the challenge is different. And there is in many cases the need to be patient, watchful – doughty. Roy is many things but he ain't Boycott.

*

How then, does Roy get the nod?

Ed Smith – Chief Selector then and until very recently - is almost a caricature of urbane intelligence. Brilliant, literary; an intimidatingly coolish bastard with the whiff of the maverick about him. Trevor Bayliss was the

---

[34] Yes. Literally. Red balls are generally used for Test cricket: they swing and move for longer than the white balls generally used for shorter formats. Different makes have different characteristics but in essence traditional red cricket balls offer more help to the bowlers than white.

(Aussie) England coach hired principally to modernize the T20 and 50 over game, following years when England were patently entrenched in a long-gone, conservative era. (In other words, he was a man for the New Positivism). James Taylor was in there as a recently retired player viewed as bright, likeable and shrewd. I would have loved – a word I'm conscious I'm over-using – to have been in the room when those selection meetings turned to how England sorts their 1/2/3.

Let's speculate – it's fun. Question One: was/is England selection *actually done* formally, as it were, with these three blokes, or their successors, plus the captain, sat around a table, at and for a prescribed time? Or is it done more via couples or threesomes meandering through the park with a coffee, or round the boundary, chewing pens? I mean we all suspect different forces come into play when things are Called to Order, yes?

Four blokes might become committee-ed in a good or bad way, perhaps. Might feel the need to perform or to defer. Might need to be blokey.

Jason Roy could only be picked to play Test cricket *and bat 1, 2 or 3* by guys either up to their necks in machismo – oh, hang on, that's all of us – or 'to do a particular job'. That job would be to swash and buckle and ideally blast the opposition either completely away, or out of their comfort zone. Roy, **we all knew**, did not have the technical game or psychological approach (otherwise known as orthodoxy) to bat high in the order in this format. So either his selection was essentially a stop-gap, or something dafter and blokier was going on.

*

Could it be that those selectors felt the pressure to be seen to be positive? That the randy, clubby alacrity of the universe got to them? After all, this is the era of the sexy and the dumb. Why wouldn't Smith, Taylor, Bayliss and Root be bounced towards bullishness? Anybody who mixes with sports coaches – or with men! - will have seen and felt the power of machismo: it can be a hoot and a rush. What it tends not to be, is thoughtful.

Of course I'm in danger of traducing Roy's talent, here, so we need to just note that a) he is a legitimate international bat b) there have been and will be plenty times when he has 'taken down' the best bowlers in the world and c) his record speaks to his quality. **This is not a diatribe against either him... or Positive Cricket.** (Really). The subtext here is about Smart Cricket, a phrase often used by Bayliss during his tenure.

To the game, briefly. A one-off, remember but still holding real import for both sides. In conditions that were tricky, certainly, for batsmen, England were dismissed for a frankly humiliating 85, in their first innings. Roy was out in the third over, for 5 runs. Ireland replied with a very gutsy 207. Then, despite being utterly undone repeatedly by Murtagh and Adair and Rankin, Roy made a crucial contribution of 72 from 78 balls, in his second knock. It was next-level streaky, a simultaneously harrowing and mesmerizing watch but combined with an extraordinary 92 from off-spinner Jack Leach it set the proverbial platform. Ireland were extinguished for 38 runs as the home side re-set the Natural Order.

Madness really had reigned, and therefore it's reckless at best to extrapolate meanings of any sort. Possible to view Roy as a hero; possible to laud Leach as the next Boycott. Watching intently, I felt some embarrassment at the obvious, prolonged discomfiture experienced by the Surrey and England dynamo. Roy was slaughtered by the Irish bowlers but somehow stayed in there. Sure, he got to 70-something but it felt more like a re-statement of the need for smart (i.e. intelligent, watchful, game-appropriate) cricket than the beginning of a new era of masculine affirmation.

Roy played a total of five Test matches, averaging 18.7 runs across his ten innings, before the experiment was closed. Was it always a temporary thing? Did the lads who did the choosing know what they were doing? Or was the ante upped by one or more of them, in an early meeting, when the positivity mantra was aired. Who might have been daft enough to say that 'we should just get Jase in there and let him express himself?' How difficult – how unmanly – to then contradict the charge?

It's one thing to have clowns like Michael Vaughan[35] (amongst many others) repeatedly fist-pumping for machismo and the dis-engagement of the brain but **this is Test Cricket** we're talking about. Michael should have noticed - and to be fair, on times, he does - that

---

[35] Former England captain, now omnipresent pundit and Twitterer – and therefore politician. With mixed results.

higher-order batting in Tests demands stickability and intelligence as well as great hands and belief. (Ideally, of course, you're looking for all four). And it's not just cricket where testosterone-fuelling is rife and unhelpful. The conflation of 'expression' with fearless male instinct is a blight on almost everything we humans do.[36]

---

[36] If there's a sentence that I'm glad to have levered into my daft wee cricket book, that's probably it.

THIRTEEN – BOWLING QUICKLY.

Ok. Literary convention[37] means I can't start this by saying "I love bowling", because I keep saying that l-word. But it's always been true, from the first moment I slung down a ball. Oh, and by the way that wouldn't have been a proper cricket ball: probably didn't feel one of those – well certainly not a new one – until I was about 12. (Could be wrong but I don't recall having the luxury of new balls to bowl with even in my first year at Secondary School. Similarly, not sure any of our gang experienced the exotic novelty and luxurious shin-protection that was cricket pads until about that same age).

Still find the feel of a Brand New Cricket Ball dreamily intoxicating, even now. Bowling is physically and metaphysically ace – who cares if that makes no sense! - particularly when done at full pelt. The movement itself, the ball, the challenge.

When we were kids we may have been neck-deep in football coaches and players but it wasn't the same for

---

[37] Not big on these: did you notice? Feels like many of these 'principles' are a way of keeping folks out/establishing hierarchies. Posh jargon is why nothing ever changes.

cricket. Or maybe we weren't really looking, being unable to see past the next game of backs and forwards. My grandad – The Mighty Vic, quick bowler as well as pro' footballer – played Minor Counties but I don't remember him ever offering any pointers.

I remember my eldest brother being described by a P.E. teacher as potentially the fastest bowler in Lincolnshire so there must have been some fraternal learning going on but (maybe wonderfully?) there was precious little external direction or instruction around. Been digging deep into retrospection: remain fascinatingly unable to picture a time when someone *actually showed us* the essential bowling movements. How great would it be if we robbed it off the telly – off Snow, Old, Botham or Holding – and free-formed our own style?

I was never an outstanding athlete but I was decent. I found a way to bowl leg-cutters at some pace. The l_v_ of it all began.

*

I've gotten closer to the game of cricket as my years have piled up. It's brought me some genuinely wonderful memories and opportunities, too. As a wandering bloggist, having remarkably been offered the privilege of ECB Accreditation, I bumped into Jimmy Anderson, at Edgbaston: it must have been Finals' Day, I think. Jimmy had fairly recently gone past the 600 wickets barrier in Test Cricket – a ludicrous number for a quick bowler. I did that embarrassing thing where I approached him in the Media Suite and delivered a corny but heartfelt congratulations. I remember it actually coming out rather well, which saved both of us some momentary grief: something of the order of

Jimmy, forgive me but I just wanted to congratulate you on your recent landmark. A lot of us have really got a lot of pleasure out of watching you bowl. Well done, mate.

Okay, hardly Churchillian but he knew I meant it – and no, he didn't have the faintest idea who I was.

So I now work in cricket – ten years as a Community Coach – and also have the privilege of swanning into Press Boxes (sometimes). This is probably why the sport-life metaphors crashing against to each other here are often wearing whites. But back to bowling.

I've heard Jimmy – a.k.a. The Burnley Express – talk elsewhere about what he does. (What he does, in case you've somehow missed it, is bewilder international batsmen). He is a truly great, skilled, top-of-the-range sportsman; maybe especially in terms of *craft*.

Anderson is tall and slim, notably so, when you stand next to him and despite the genuine perils of his trade – in which physical breakdown is common – has typically stayed fit, over an extraordinary, long career. Like Bumrah, perhaps, he is neither a powerhouse nor intimidating by the standards of the day. He has a snarky competitive spirit, occasionally roused but doesn't feel like he could or would *actually* beat you up, unlike one or two of his colleagues in the fast-bowling community. And he's simply not *that* quick – just quick enough. Anyway, back to what he's said: soon.

Jimmy *swings* the ball, meaning he can get it to curl or move 'off-line', in the air. This is of course not unusual for an international bowler, but Anderson does it big... and does it both ways; what we call in and out-swingers. His gift is the degree to which he can control that sphere as it swings in those two directions and the awesome repeatability of his skills.

A new cherry-red cricket ball, particularly of the Duke's variety (as opposed to the less responsive Kookaburra) can be steered into swinging and deceiving or unsettling the batsman. **Exercising control** of a hard, new, red cricket ball, with its fast and slow side (from shining/not shining) really is an art, of which Anderson has probably been the leading exponent, arguably world-wide, for the last ten years or more.

But how does he do it? Let me briefly transpose the sense of the online master classes Anderson has run.

- He shines the ball and 'looks after it' – that is tries to buff it up and keep *one side* in pristine condition, during the match. He will expect the same of his fielders.[38]

---

[38] Most international teams now have a particular individual fielder responsible for the condition of the ball. It's become BIG, in a marginal gains kindofaway. Which means abuses – such as the infamous 'Sandpapergate' (Australia guilty, v South Africa, in 2018) – are probably inevitable, despite acute regulation.

- (To bowl his trademark away-swinger from the right-handed batsman) Anderson sets the seam of the ball relatively upright... but in fact pointing towards 3rd or 4th slip – that is, ten o'clockish - during delivery.

- If the batsman is a right-hander, the shiny side of the ball will be on the *inside,* (i.e. facing the leg-side of the pitch), as Anderson releases. (If you're still not sure what this means, think *behind the batsman,* as he stands square-on, to the bowler).

- Jimmy then looks to impart just a touch of back-spin onto the ball, by keeping fingers one and two (as it were) in contact until the last millisecond. He talks about having a very light grip, so the ball is almost floating from the hand. *Feel* is as important as power, or pace.

- For in-swingers, the shiny side will face towards off, the seam will aim towards leg-slip – two o'clock - and the touch of the fingers will be marginally shifted, to assist the subtly amended steer. But hey, this is no exact science. This is magic. Individual magic.

What's notable and *effective* is that Anderson can do this with a calm but relentless accuracy. He has a classical, grooved action which we might otherwise regard as unremarkable. That repeatability and something wonderfully personal to him, in the finer movements, have turned a quietish, outwardly slightly dour human into one of the gods of sport. How gently gorgeous that we can't entirely unpick his secret?

*

Some time ago I spent some hours with Dr James Scobie, of Bath University, who is an expert on the mechanics of – you guessed it – **swing bowling**. I met him briefly at my son's reconnaissance mission pre-entry, and set up a full-on interview and, inevitably in the era of Lookie Here, a podcast, recorded in September 2018. In the hope that some of you non-cricket people present might nevertheless be wondering at the cosmic forces involved around how spheres deviate through the atmosphere, I'm going to blast through a few of his key findings. Because we're beyond sport here and into the Science of Wonder, yes?

There is a kind of assumption, in the cricket community – o-kaaaay, if there is such a thing – that the ball swings 'when it's muggy'. Test Matches in late summer at Trent Bridge or Headingley; cloud; 'first thing' – i.e. 10.30 or 11 am. Or it 'starts hooping' as a hint of duskiness descends. Principally, there is an association with some damp and the generation of swing. Not true, or not that simple, says the doc.

We have to be careful with terminology, here. So I will quote Dr Scobie directly, as he clarifies this question:

"Humidity in isolation has no effect".

Scobie had done prolonged experiments where (amongst other things) he incrementally increased the level of humidity inside wind tunnels in which balls were subjected to different air-flows, to replicate speed and movement. Increasing the presence of water in the atmosphere did not affect levels of swing.

Look out, here comes some science:

"What we are arguing is that in order to cause the ball to swing you need the asymmetry set up by laminar flow on one side of the ball and turbulent flow on the other. If the environment is not conducive to this then swing will not occur".

Clear as mud? Well let's try to demystify – although in doing that also *holler from the rooftops* that Dr Scobie happily concedes that some of this stuff 'remains a mystery'. Regarding that mugginess argument, it remains contentious with people in the game. I wonder if the relatively cool **stillness** on those days is closer to the centre of the issue: certainly turbulence above the strip caused by re-radiated heat (in Aus and India, for example) may mitigate against swing.

Imagine a cricket ball fixed in a wind-tunnel, within which pressure, air-flow, humidity are controllable and measurable. (The wind-tunnel I saw at Bath Uni was in an office-sized room, with the essential gubbins – I'm sure they call it that – about twenty feet long). Note that the ball can be removed, to affect its condition, if helpful and can be re-fixed so as to present the seam at a different perspective to the air-flow (or wind).

Seam position is critical.

Despite being a mere two or three milimetres proud of the otherwise spherical shape of the ball, the seam has a profound effect on movement through the air. Why? Friction, in a word: air flow, in two. If the ball has a shiny side *laminar flow* – we can think of this as smoothish and uninterrupted – will occur as air passes around it. The combination of an outcropping seam and a relatively rough surface on the *other hemisphere* will create *turbulent flow* here. In short, the differences between these two types of air flow may facilitate swing because the shiny side can move marginally more quickly through the air than the worn side: the ball arcs, because of that uneven relationship. Much of the rest is down to skill – to feel.

There have been great swing bowlers for a hundred years. There have been theories for decades – including that of Dr Scobie. I'm sure Jimmy Anderson knows about this laminar flow/turbulent flow dichotomy and can process some of the science but I'm guessing that he's not really that bothered about the astonishingly fine measurements or let's face it, the medium-dense Fluid Dynamics theories pertaining. He just runs in and tries to steer the ball with the seam. Then the enchantment begins.

FOURTEEN - FIELDING POINT.

Maybe I should have put the fact that I don't like it when cricketers at any level say they can't stand fielding into BAD STUFF IN THE GAME(S). Because that does get on my wick.

Apart from stating the obvious – everybody has to field – it seems such a miserable disposition. You can't be a team man or woman if you don't field. You can't contribute, get better or do yourself, your team or the game justice if you don't field whole-heartedly. Okay I get that some of the folks who say they can't stand fielding will do so brilliantly and with commitment through their gritted teeth but... *how can you enjoy cricket if you don't switch on in the field?*

Trying to make sense of this. A further, brief, non-scientific rummage through my own experience suggests that it's most often higher-order batters that can't stand fielding. Would the related Venn diagram also place these people in the subset 'Likely to be Miserable Bastards, Generally', I wonder? (Did Morrissey field, or dip out, at school? I hear Joe Strummer was a demon cover point).

Is a sort of narrow-eyed self-obsession more likely to occur in Top, Top Batters? Possibly. Are stats available on this? Not yet, I imagine. I'm troubled by this stuff. Is the genius of sport not something connected to revelling in shared purpose, or did I just say something hilariously retro again?

The thing is fielding is great. Chasing down that disappearing ball. Watching *forever* with an accumulating panic as a skier descends theoretically within your grasp. Catching – or dropping. Diving. Setting your feet and flinging down the wickets. The keeper's #bantz. Everybody's #bantz. That range of noisy, matey encouragement or icy, concentrated calm. The eruptions after a wicket.

I remember talking to the brilliant Cricket Man, coach and Coach Educator Jeremy Cartwright about this: how he really liked his teams to be quiet. That spoke of course of his own character and possibly generation – which, incidentally, is mine. I think his rationale was coupled to a belief in powerful and possibly austere concentration. Minds being fixed for sustained periods in which communion was more telepathic than verbal. Words being superfluous. All the necessary team dynamism coming from sharp movement and sharp focus – from anticipation and execution; from understanding.

Still find this idea interesting and recognise some real merit... but it feels less applicable now. Maybe that's the dumbing-down of the universe impinging yet again, who knows? Everything being urgent, and/or unquiet. What is beyond dispute is that levels of agility, energy and ambition in the field are generally massively higher than they were twenty or thirty years ago. And this is good.

That increased fizz, charge and athleticism in professional cricketers is driven by many things. The players are *conditioned* in a way that Gower, Botham and co might even have refused to contemplate. Not just Beep Tests and burpees but hours of programmed 'S & C',[39] individually tailored to get players ver-ry fit... and fit for their roles.

Fine conditioning is now a non-negotiable. The days of fast bowlers not diving and Mike Gatting[40] not running are gone. (Contraflow. There may be a minor negative, here, if there is no longer a place for a brilliant porker. But now that T20 is god and every ball must be stopped, few professionals are going to be voracious pie-eaters. And mostly this reflects into sexier, zestier, more watchable cricket).

Not all fielding is better but watch any short-format event and you will see that routinely the game is more intensely and/or consistently alive, across the oval, than at any time. Set aside if you can any concerns about faux carnivalism or naff, insta-tribalism. The cricket fielding spectacle itself, irrespective of coloured clobbah and forced jubilation, is more entertaining *in this respect*: players are diving/catching/launching/parrying to partners from beyond the boundary. That energy is

---

[39] Strength and Conditioning. Unheard of last Wednesday week, essential today.

[40] *Solidly-built* former England skipper.

good; is healthy. We can separate this argument from issues around 'baseballification'.[41]

*

My teams tend to be noisy in a way that I hope is supportive. I don't like sledging and I don't like dishonesty: call me a sad git but I hope my players would walk. I encourage my players to support each other, often using the idea that first *and foremost* "we're a gang of mates". So it's good for Danny to leg it twenty yards to slap Rhys on the back, after a great stop, or for the skipper to keep positive vibes tripping round the outfield – as long as we don't delay the game and we pipe down during play. Hugs and high-fives can feel essential, can *be* essential if your best bowler's having a bad day but then flukes a wicket.

The **humour** of a team and the volume of **good energy** flowing around and between its players can be important: if it's natural (whatever that is) for Sioned and Carys to bounce around and offer a joyful squeeze, then surely let them do it? It can *work*: I absolutely believe that you can express your superiority as a team as well as your togetherness, by how you field. The collective effort, the determined, respectful process can be the provider. More importantly, for me, it can be bloody rewarding – and *enjoyable*.

*

---

[41] Some would argue that T20 and the Hundred mean cricket is edging ever closer to baseball: i.e. it's a slogathon.

There is something of a tradition that you put your best fielder – that is, your most agile, your sharpest – at point or cover point. Could be this is less prevalent today, as (stat-driven) ever-more sophisticated **bowling plans** become central. Bowlers may now target a very specific weakness which will force the batter to try to hit a particular shot to a particular place: this may mean point and cover point are relatively idle. But let's return to that historical idyll.

The thinking was that quickish bowling of a natural length and line is likely to finish up here, in the cover point to backward point zone, when struck. (Point is at 90 degrees to the line of the delivery, 'square' of the wicket, in front of the batter's chest; typically twenty-something yards away. Cover point is forward of this towards the bowler). Because quick bowlers slam it down there, batters often play *late* (as opposed to out in front of themselves) and the ball is therefore cut or driven, sometimes off the back foot, to this sector of the outfield.

If you're standing at point or cover point, best keep your hands warm; you're gonna get some stingers. Be ready to throw yourself left or right. Pace on the ball from the bowler translates readily into pace off the bat. So you're frequently in the business of stopping boundaries. It's a matter of pride as well as a key part of the contest.

Jonty Rhodes, the South African phenomenon prowled this area with predatory distinction in the nineties (mainly), arguably ushering in the new era of dynamism in the field. Inevitably Rhodes progressed into coaching fielding, where his urgency and inspirational qualities combine with his extravagant reputation, knowledge and experience. He is mad for foot speed and awareness. Having been an outstanding hockey player and footballer, he understood and valued early, the significance of all-round athleticism and agility.

Rhodes was widely regarded as the best male fielder of all time. Today, there are three or four players at every major T20 franchise who are fielding close to his level. And everybody else is being stretched - sometimes literally – towards his astonishing standards.

In the women's game, players are being similarly challenged, conditioned and developed towards higher standards: increased professionalism is of course key to this, bringing as it does a whole new level of expectation. The Non-negotiables extend. For England, Fran Wilson and Danni Wyatt are amongst those whose dynamism and ambition in the field is consistently excellent. It feels important to me (as someone coaching in girls' pathways) that the elite players are throwing themselves around. Sends a great message about athleticism, the throwing off of self-consciousness... and it's part of the fun, right?

*

Fielding is like everything else in that your intent counts. And as per any other team activity bonding and commitment may not guarantee success but they will make it more likely.

Those feel like *statements* – like essential truths – but does that make them facts? Should we coach them as such? It seems reasonable, seems like there is even a healthy imperative towards engagement, commitment, togetherness in there. If things are organically communicated in whatever way, then we might expect that confidence and encouragement must surely play a part in a winning culture, yes?

But can 'teaminess' also go the other way? For example, despite our psychological revelation around individual, possibly controllable events, spilled catches really do feel like they breed spilled catches: us cricketers have all experienced that horrendous infection running through our sides. Is that team failure or individual failure? And how do we address it?

Ooh. Did I just say winning culture? And should that be in the Corporate Bollocks column from chapter whatever-it-was? (Deep breath and conclude, bois-bach, deep breath and con-clude).

I like the words energy and readiness. Ready positions and that whole unweighting thing, I like. Physically and mentally, get yourself primed. Get ready to do your bit. Field.

FIFTEEN - A DAY IN THE LIFE OF (A COMMUNITY COACH).

School day? Despite recent challenges, let's assume so. Let's assume some historical normalcy. Maybe, with that in mind, I'll base this around something from September 2020, when I was a regular working guy.

Up at ten to seven. Being one of those annoying bar-steds who reach maximum revs about three minutes after waking, I'm on it, alarmingly pronto - productive. De-populate the bladder, wash hands and face: warm water. Then in our house it's always the washing-up pile. (Just me, or do most of you lot wake up to half an hour's clattering and swishing of 'pots?' Or are the majority dishbloodywasher-owners, these days? Would be mildly interested in the stats on that. Am I crazy thinking that one of the reasons you have kids is to eventually draw up a sink-side rota?)[42]

Not being a martyr but it's me who does them in our house, ninety percent of the time. And most mornings

---

[42] We had a washing-up rota, as kids. Long before dishwashers but whatever. Oh and hey – just me, or do the plates and wotnots really stink, when they come out of a dishwasher? Punishment of Luxury, maybe...

there really is best part of thirty minutes of dunking and wiping to be done, or was when we had a full team out – or at home. (One now dispatched to Bath Uni, as you've heard). This is not entirely a moan, mind, because *this time* somehow manages to be thinking time as well as a sort of sumptuous brain-deathville. I will be contemplating the day ahead, visualizing, Steve Smith-like, the challenge that Year 2/3 might put in front of me. I might even be twitchily scraping my feet around in the crease beneath the bowl.

My wife being The Finest Yoga Teacher in Wales, we eat organic porridge with blueberries, walnuts and a smidge of cold milled flaxseed, for brekkie. Rice or oat milk, of course. I make that in between the washing and wiping. We alternate somewhat, around that school pack-up for the kid(s) dilemma. Wraps? A box of 'P & T' – pasta, pesto and tuna - or buy there? (I will be taking something for me: this last winter I got into a helpfully minimalist groove, where I was eating only oatcakes and a chunk of cucumber at work, plus maybe a banana. Plus water. Weirdly, that worked fine for me for several weeks, although I was only going in on three days: to electrify the feasting experience I might on occasion take a wee pot of pickle).

Always a briefish dog walk but this means I yomp *every morning* to the cliff top and the Pembrokeshire Coast Path, often brew or even porridge in hand, to facilitate the pooch's evacuations and to inhale, wonderfully deeply, the salty gale or restorative calm. Every blessed day.

I would be leaving home, during this period, just after eight, allowing me slack time for the hassle of getting into school car parks. Sometimes, maybe particularly in these Covid times, when access is controlled, you can get snagged. I always like time to *set up*, think, be calm and ready.

*

We work to a kind of curriculum but also not. My employers, Cricket Wales and their funders Chance to Shine train us well and guide or provide us (and the schools, obviously) with a schedule of activities but do I think also trust us to edit or add to the material. After all, we not only have experience but we are 'in the room', which we can and must read. Part of how this works *needs to be* coach tweaking and amending, to make sessions appropriate to the group and the moment.

Much as I'd like to big up some fine people and a fine school, it may be a tad more professional to leave out names and some other details, as we go on. Yaknow, *reasons*. Let's get in there.

I arrive at a biggish Primary School by Pembrokeshire's standards, for the first day of delivery. Prior to this is I had held an informal 'Induction' with the Deputy Head, in order to thrash out a plan and sign off risk assessments etc. (Yes, there is some admin: but goodwill and a pre-existing relationship means this is swiftly and painlessly dealt with. In fact we are mates and he is as pleased to have me back in the school as I am delighted to be there).

It could be because this is Pembrokeshire and I've been doing this for ten years but this tends to be the way of it. Often mutual respect; often some real friendship. Fabulous, supportive environment. There will be six weekly visits: I will deliver six sessions per day to classes from Years 2 and 3. I will have a teacher or an assistant supporting on each occasion.

A whole day of coaching – six sessions of about 50 minutes, give or take – is pretty intense but Covid has dictated a slight swerve in this direction. To minimize mixing and travelling, I am planting my feet in one school for a whole day, rather than the more traditional flitting between two. The particular day I am about to describe was in fact the *first bundle of sessions possible*, after the Covid/summer holidays combo had intervened.

*

Kit. We haven't mentioned it and if I'm to describe some of the hows, here, maybe it might be relevant – interesting, even, for some?

Firstly I am well aware of the coaching incantation that says something along the lines of 'the more cones you lay out, the less of a coach you are'. In other words, experience and knowledge and adaptation count, not kit. Some truth in that – deffo. But I carry a lot of clobber around with me... and leave some of it in the car, depending on the plan, the weather, what the location feels like.

There *is* a plan. Chance to Shine have worked up a genuinely excellent scheme, which I have (as a kind of intellectual/theoretical challenge) tried hard to stick pretty close to, in recent months. So for example in our first sessions, we are all 'Cool Catchers'. There are drills for me to follow. I choose to do that - more than I was – but inevitably these don't always suit, or catch the vibe. I re-calibrate and re-invent constantly to keep the energy and engagement high. But we've drifted from kit.

We are supplied with everything we need, from our black Cricket Wales/Chance to Shine trackies, caps and shorts, to the bats, balls, cones and markers we use in play. I've added in the odd teddy, hoop and BIG Bright Shiny Ball or two to draw in the un-confident or differently-abled. A range of tactile as well as visual experiences can be surprisingly enriching *to all*, though, yes?

This first day – 15th September, 2020 - after donning mask, signing in and marching through the corridors and out to the dampish, lush-ish field, I took almost everything I own. (No indoor space available: had to make it work, somehow. Grass was longish, meaning balls were never going to bounce or roll much). Had spent plenty of time watching 'Cool Catchers' videos, soaking up the broader material and (absolutely) rehearsing what I'd say and do - much of this whilst standing at that sink and/or driving schoolwards. Okay the ground conditions were medium-unwelcoming, the kids I knew would be boisterous but I was definitely ready.

Four sets of bats and stumps; giant bag stuffed with maybe five different biggish balls, hoops and tees, tennis racket, teddy and sponge balls – the latter for indoor use, mainly. Oh – and cones and marking discs. Bucket of tennis and wind-balls, with a few beanbags and soft-but-spiky balls in there, for variety. Sanitizer spray and hand-gel. Plus a satchel containing diary, notepad, ipad, water and those scrunched-up bits of paper from 2006.

*

Here's something. Us Community Coaches are looking to do more than just get kids into our particular game. As well as enthusing youngsters for cricket here's a few of the things that are rattling round my brain *during sessions*.

- Are these kids buzzing, yet?
- How are they, listening-wise?
- How much time, if any, am I going to spend trying to get Jonny the Lunatic back into this?
- Did I make Sara laugh? (Think I might need to). She's not looking like she's joined us.
- Are these kids able to throw in worthwhile suggestions, re- our warm-up? Could that be fun, could that be helpful, to ask? Or would they fanny about, too much, or just be 'too young?'
- Are these movements yaknow – *invigorating?*
- Am I talking too much? Did I let that game run long enough? What's the natural length of that exercise? Does it *really* lead into what I was planning... or do I need a swerve, sharpish?
- Are we demonstrating to the universe (and that teacher) that I'll be offering a challenge to the kids' attention? And that we'll move that on, to *really*

ask questions of their ability to work in pairs, in groups?

- Am I over-thinking this and not letting these kids *just play?*
- Is this both great fun and **much more than cricket? Because it should be.**

*

I set up a very simple area with two straightish, twenty-odd metre-long lines of cones, about twelve to fifteen metres apart: this to accommodate the group – of towards thirty Year 3's – in-bound. We were going to warm-up and get to know each other by doing 'journeys' across this space.

Because I have quite a bundle of experience and because I neither mind making an arse of myself nor fear needing to backtrack or change, I tend not to be nervous about holding court to new playmates. I think I have some faith that my half-decent humour and capacity to *get things moving* will make things work, well enough. Plus the sight of a familiar teacher leading out the group helped. I knew from previous visits that she a) completely gets it and b) she will be outstandingly supportive – appreciative, even.

I do brief introductions in a way that makes clear that our relationship can be different to that which prevails between kids and staff: I'm 'not one of your teachers'. I loosen it up, make it clear that laughs are o-kaay, as long as we're respectful; and yes I do use that word. But I throw the lecturing away early-doors and we're off

– moving – to the Finest Jog of All Time. Two journeys! Let's go!!

Dafydd hasn't listened so he's off into his third and beyond. Eleri was slowish but it's not yet clear if she's attention-seeking or if her Whole-body Movements lack fluency. 'Miss' is already mopping up the drifters in a fair but persistent way. Nearly everyone's giggling. This is gonna be great.

*

I have fifty minutes with these kids. I want movement and catching, essentially. As I'd hoped, the children *did* suggest, on invitation, some of the activity, even early-on. *"C'mon guys, who's seen Gareth Bale? Who's seen the rugby men and women or the swimmers, on the telly? What do they do, what can we do, that might be fun and get us ready for the games?"* So getting minds active as well as feet.

I loved that as the suggestions built, one boy wheeled his arms rather unconvincingly in what looked like a weakish front crawl. I slung in some real encouragement and we turned it into two different, legitimately active journeys. The first we walked briskly forward but *really front-crawled like in the Olympics*; the second we went backwards, wheeling our arms and opening our chests 'like a Wales flanker might, just before the England game'. Instead of drowning, that lad was beaming. We had extended the meaning, length and value of the warm-up significantly. We'd jogged, hopped, 'bounced', skipped sideways, sprinted, shaken out our hands and feet, done Backstroke Rugby and *combined these movements over 1/2/3 or 4 journeys,* to test or engage our listening, resilience, memory, co-ordination. Time to try some catching.

Everybody gets their own ball and I ask for twelve catches, in two journeys. Don't say anything about what kind of catches; just say I want exactly twelve, please. (I know most will forget that bit. I know some will sling the ball waaay too high but the balls are soft so no-one will get hurt – there'll just be a little anarchy and excitement. Sometimes that's great and I can reign it in if need be). I sit back, as it were and watch, secretly hoping that some sharp cookie might move one yard, throw twelve catches immediately, then sprint home. Nobody does.

Of course I could demonstrate some catching and indeed at some stage I will. But maybe the learning experience is richer – maybe – if we have a few tries and perhaps check out our pals a bit, before I ask the class to 'coach me?'

Ok friends, so imagine... if I was an alien, who'd just landed... and I was watching the game... what suggestions might you make to help me join in... and make some catches? How are we making this work?

Get a range of answers. (There'll always be a couple of kids who a) can do the sports-thing and b) are the strong characters who always get heard. Don't just call in with them, eh?) If you ask a child who seems unsure or lacking in confidence you can always ease them to the direction you want to go: just **hear them.** Keep the questions coming: *'so we get ready; what does that look like? And two hands, maybe together like a bowl or nest?'* To the inevitable *'you've got to watch the ball'* I might add (and perhaps demonstrate whilst I'm doing so) that **when you were making it work, you watched the ball all... the way... in.**

Often, because it both makes them laugh and genuinely tends to support execution, I bring out the elephant. By this I mean that at the exact moment that the ball (which is being ferociously watched, right?) is successfully gathered into the hands, I say the word 'elephant' **out loud, whilst keeping my eyes fixed, on that ball, in those hands.** It's a way of maintaining the watch... all the way in... and beyond. (Most catches are dropped because the ball isn't truly followed right through that last, critical phase: we 'take our eye off it'). This is a bit of fun that reinforces that learning.

*

Catching to me feels like a life-skill as much as a game: bit like throwing, in that regard. Get the hang of these things early and a zillion games/adventures/successes become possible. With youngish kids – and maybe not-so-young? – this fixing of the head and eyes is a good skill to register. Heads are massive, in sport. Final note; strictly for the lols, I often let kids insert their own word, here. Can be hilarious... and liberating, somehow.

*

So, we've found ourselves catching. Moving, as a group, now doing those journeys with or without our elephants but catching on our own. I've effectively added in This Month's Mantra – *"How do we make this work?"* – by asking the kids to help out that passing alien. I'm trying to find a way of getting encouragement and maybe a technical nugget or two into the faces of every individual in the group, if possible. (Not that easy, with a two-metre Covid exclusion-zone being factored in). I'm also now looking to step into Mantra 2 territory, by asking *"how do we make this fun?"*

But let me step back, briefly. Of all the things that have stayed with me throughout the reasonably extensive Coach Education I've received, over many years, there's this: the idea that making eye contact with (and more than that – actually *seeing* and *acknowledging*) every player in your care during every session **is powerful.** Happy to name and credit the indomitable Peter Brett for this. Peter is a brilliant, authoritative, technical coach, based in Wales who has worked at a significantly higher stratum in the game than I ever will. We're very different people: it makes me laugh that we are at polar extremes politically but still manage to rub along – admittedly mainly on Twitter!

I think he dropped this particularly generous notion into my ECB Level Two course, donkeys years ago. "Get through to everybody. Value everybody". Peter seems like a rather robust individual: felt good and still does that someone at his level would still be stressing the importance of *personal contact* - and meaning it. I carry that with me. You hear a lot of glib stuff from coaches (or organisations) about making their players into better people. For me, this **contact** is like a baseline, a starting point for all parties.

*

But back in our session we need variety and we need ideas, ideally from the children. I start asking what else we can add in, to make it make it more of a challenge, or more fun. Could be that I make the first suggestion but this will depend on the group. We make journeys, adding in claps, bounces – despite these being tricky on the grass. In time we're adding in specific numbers of both, plus some 'basketball skills' and/or 'high, HIGH ones'. Half an hour or so in, and time for a break-out.

*

I carry about ten hoops and a dozen flat, circular markers with me. I place them out front and describe quite carefully what we're going to do. *"We're going to think about how to make this fun"*. The children now have to find a partner and choose either a hoop or a marker and *go anywhere in the field* (within reason) and make up a game for two. They can only use one ball, at this stage. It takes a couple of minutes for partners to be sorted – by them, not me – and balls to be chosen or rejected but most of them burst away purposefully.

The teacher gets that we're trying to challenge the kids to co-operate, organize and *create new games*, here. And that there are some minor risks, in terms of children faffing about, losing interest or being lazy, as they are the ones now doing all the heavy lifting. But we can wander around and offer a little encouragement, or recognize some great work, or fabulous thinking. So we do. What we try not to do is tell them, or direct them.

With a slightly heavy heart I have had to instruct for no 'long-distance' throwing of the hoops. They *do fly* and I have seen kids get sliced. But (as the children soon discover) they can be held up, as targets, or thrown up just a little, as well as placed on the floor. Looking around, it's clear that throwing is as key as catching, now. Fine. We are making games and some of them are really working.

I let this run for what feels like a long time – because there is value in the fumble towards compromise, viability and fun. The arguing or sharing, the 'trying things out'. The spark of creation and the bark of disagreement. #Lifesrichwotnots.

As I walk around I am thinking:

- those two lads are gonna sling that ball over the fence.
- Look at these girls, with their catches. Adding claps and *street moves!*
- Might ask matey boy over here what we could change... to make it more fun.
- Anybody still bringing out their elephant?
- Would love to do a full-on Strictly Come Catching game (involving bounce-catches and dance-moves or tricks) but the grass is too bloody lush for an

activity where timing around the bouncing ball is so central). Will park that 'til we get on the playground.

- Do I show these guys my three paces thing? More a throwing game than catching. Do I need to save that up for next week?
- Tell you what, that feels long enough. Let's gather in and talk.

Okaaay team. I've loved seeing so many different games going on out there. Who can tell me what they added in to the catching to make it more fun? Who had a great idea? Who had something that nearly worked but they had to change it?

Brief discussion, where one or two things are reported; changes in throw and distance, hoop as target, clapping routines, dance-moves and cartwheels between catches. Somebody grasses-up Dylan, for launching the markers. Importantly, the **children recount stuff that worked.** The majority of action might have been messy and inconclusive but they have learned a bit about what they might add, to make a game fun.

*

We've had a relatively challenging period in the session, where the kids have known they're supposed to be thinking, as well as chucking things around. I reckon, and I know from a very brief chat with the teacher that she agrees, that it was legitimate. There was fun, there was movement and there was enough purpose. I want to close out by getting these kids buzzing again:

wouldn't always do this because sending them back to class on a high can be unhelpful to the class teacher but it feels strongly, instinctively the right thing to do. We go back to our original area and our catching and without mentioning the word race, we fizz through a few more journeys.

I have upped the energy and the encouragement to make it feel like a laugh: you can do that. Most kids love to move if you get in there with them and scatter some cheer around the place. Could be that if you pitch it right you can simultaneously raise the quality of attention, too. So I buzz with them, for them, to support them. We add in claps – one, two, three, four! – and then go for our own Personal Best!

C'mon, people. How many claps can we get in, with our catch, if we throw this high? (Three metres). And how many now... when it's THIS HIGH?!? (Ten metres).

Maybe we finish with that whiff of anarchy but we absolutely finish smiling. Last word.

*Dear friends I'm not really here to give you marks out of ten. But that was **twenty-five** out of ten. (It genuinely was). So what a great session!*

I think you might hear a couple of questions from me quite a lot, over the next six weeks. Those questions might be 'how do we make this work' – in other words what do we do to help with our catching; how do we hold our hands, do we bring out the elephant, maybe? And also 'how do we make this fun?' Not how does

Rick the daft cricket-man-fella make this fun: 'how do we make this fun?'

Okay. Can you please do that thing where you line up beautifully and go back into class quietly with your teacher. Thank you. And well done. Fantastic start.

*

It had been a fantastic start. The dangerous bit or ambitious bit where the kids were left to invent (or argue and sling the balls over the fence) went ver-ry well. There were some lively – that is, potentially disruptive individuals - in this posse and the session gripped most of them, most of the time. The teacher gave me a generous thankyou before marching them off: in fact better than that, she rather skillfully invited the children to offer their thanks. First session, twenty-five out of ten: five more in the day.

*

In between sessions I had about ten minutes to sanitize kit – this I did by spraying every ball used or item of clobber handled – and gather my thoughts. I had about sixty balls available so tried to alternate in the ones unused in the previous session: not an absolutely bullet-proof system but then appropriate (and the best we could do) given whole-class bubbles were in operation. Covid at this time was relatively rare in Pembrokeshire.

The remainder of the day went well. I used similar themes but varied games and timing of things. Maybe I asked more of Year 3 than 2 – hard to be specific on that due to the passage of time and the individual nature of the groups and the wee humans wandering in. I had about twenty minutes genuine break over lunch so inevitably it was relatively demanding of my energy and focus but after that flying start I knew I was back in the groove. I'd re-found that Receptively Urgent Mode and delivered some half-decent lessons. Later, think I prob'ly slept okay, too, after best part of six hours out in the coolish, dampish air.

SIXTEEN – PALATE CLEANSER.

You know that thing where you just feel like you need to swish things out? Yeh, that.

If I had some of the vodka I once tried, at a Christmas Market – at Picton Castle, if you know it? – I'd be going for that. Made out of cucumber, by some crafty-looking geezer with a beard. Cool and yeh, cucumbery but not tricksy and weird, like some of that artisan booze stuff. 32 quid a bottle but you could see why, somehow. I'd be going with that. Straight. Maybe with ice.

What's yours?

SEVENTEEN – A KIND OF ECSTASY.

More coaching: discretion needed so forgive the generality of some of this. I wish I felt freer to name the kids and the teachers involved.

I went to coach at a school with a 'unit'. Meaning something vaguely different/'challenging'/unknowable. I was primed in the sense that an exchange of emails with a teacher I knew in the school alluded to that specialism, via acronym – as is often the way, in our various industries. Thing was, I knew the acronym meant 'unit' but not much more. I did not recognize the particular letters punched out alongside the timing for that particular lesson.

So when I turned up (for what we call an Engagement Day), I asked.

Dude, forgive my ignorance, but what's the deal with the guys at 10 'til 11ish?

My comrade answered rather fully, perhaps even intimidating himself a little with his barrage of apologies for the Things That Might Not Happen, But Don't Worry. After the flurry, I promised it would be fine, surprisingly calmly.

I felt calm, despite being told that X may not even make it out to join us, because he's so disruptive and restless and Y is well, similar. And Z will drift and maybe 'kick off'. The briefing in short was professional and necessary: not least because this was the first time in ten years of coaching in schools that I have been told the nine children joining me would have and need five teachers to support.

Wow. I think I felt that was kinda exciting and fascinating as well as yaknow... quite a prospect. Five teachers. Nine kids. Unthinkable luxury in different – i.e. 'normal' circumstances.

A Year 4 group preceded, which may have given me the opportunity to get in the groove. After a genuinely uplifting and engaging session with them, I closed out by thanking them and wondering

if you could do that thing where you line up beautifully wherever teacher thinks is good... and then go back inside helpfully quietly, please.

They did. It was great. All of it. I sanitized the clobber, imagining there would be a few minutes gap, but soonish – sooner than I thought, though I felt ready – X and probably Y came gamboling around the corner.

The amorphous 'group' were ambling or meandering or charging, a little. They were manifestly not 'lined up'. I watched as they walked/lumbered/wheeled, extravagantly, the fifty yards or so towards me. (Did I say I was on the mugger? Multi-use Games Area, I think, although this could well be another acronym I haven't nailed. Decent, but coarse-ish tarmac surface). I noted, naturally, that my colleague wasn't exaggerating when he talked about the staff/pupil ratio... but no alarms. Boisterous, yes, some, and maybe not that *aware*, or focused, the first arrivals, but friendly enough. No confrontational stuff in the ether. Boys and girls – mainly boys.

I don't have many times quite like these but when waiting on or welcoming incoming groups it feels right to try to exude the right stuff - though again, I don't over-think this. Friendly, first and foremost; interested *in them*. Solid. Authentic. So I talk in the usual daft, welcoming, non-teachery way, setting the boundaries somewhere pleasingly different. As I ask them to gather on my magic yellow line I am making it clear non-verbally – how else? - that a Shouty Policeman I am not. It's gonna be more fun than that.

*

One or two of these children are smiling at this potentially bonkers bloke already: one or two have their heads down or away but I am absolutely not going to pre-judge their ability to listen, interact, or get busy in a sporting stylee. Completely instinctively (probably) I go again with a warm-up that only really works if they buy in and (as well as doing the movements) do some thinking. We'll know ver-ry soon if this is asking too much, or – as I hope – it'll get their antennae twitching positively. Like mine.

OK friends, I know some of you have seen Aaron Ramsey, or your favourite swimmer or cricketer or rugby player on the telly... before their matches, or events. But what are they doing, I wonder? (Am-dram quizzical face).

They are doing a warm-up... and I want us to do a warm-up together, strictly for the lols... and because then we're really going to be ready to play some cricketty games.

I want you to help me out with this. I'll get us started but then I am going to ask you for some ideas, some movements. Things we might do to get us buzzing and prepared.

RIGHT, COME ON. I'm going to call a trip across the playground a journey; can we have two journeys, please, using the Finest Jog This Village Has Ever Seen? [43] *Let's do it!*

They do. I am moving a little, too, in and out, encouraging, confirming, where necessary that this is indeed, the Finest Jog This Village Has Ever Seen. I am watchful. They are jogging, most of them, with a certain but differentiated glee. Wonderfully. Some needing to work at even this; some unselfconsciously in their flow. Critically they have all understood the daft but liberating mission here, already. We're kinda mates, already.

---

[43] Yup. Recycled – as, inevitably, is a fair bit of the routine. But it's a funny, unthreatening and appropriate way in.

I offer two more movements; firstly 'sideways crabbing' for **four journeys,**

with journeys one and three facing thissaway... and two and four facing thissaway. Huh?

(I turn and make scrambled-brain face, so that they know this is a ridiculously complex ask. Or is it?) Again there is understanding and eagerness; smiles, as they are **switching on.** The range of movement is notable – from fully coordinated stepping to assisted, lumpen, unconvincing shuffles. The teachers are in there supporting and I'm happily building the energy:

yes, X, that's the wildest, free-est, most crabtastic sideways pincer-thing I've ever seen! Yes Z, and hang on, did I see you at the last Crab Olympics? Outstanding, people!

Now we need to change. What are we going to call this one?

(*I demonstrate high knees*).

Let's do two journeys with high knees!

(If I'm over-dosing on the exclamation marks here, forgive me; I was en-bloody-couraging to the max, so the vibe was noisy-ish and upful. We all do this differently but this is my way – energy up, enthusiasm high).

The children **respond.** When I get them back to the magic line and ask for ideas... we get ideas. Jumping.

Hopping. Running – meaning flat out. I fine-tune the suggestions but value them all and thank their originators. (By now I have most of the names. Often I wouldn't but here it's possible and I figure if I can single these kids out for extravagant praise every now and again, they might thrive on that. Oh – and they do).

We often *freestyle* the suggestions. I am calling the kids 'coach' and I ask their permission for their mates to add lib.

Okay coach I am loving this jumping idea. If you're comfortable with this, I'm going to ask you to set off just ahead of the rest of The Posse and demonstrate your movements. Then the other guys can either follow your pattern, or add something in – something jumpy. You okay with that, coach?

They were. They did both. Some were tortuous but all tried like hell... and all made it across the journeys. Their ideas and their ability to communicate – in different ways, at different levels – was magic, was fascinating and it was a further reminder never to pre-judge anybody. (Z threw me, I confess, when he said something different-level insightful about warm-ups, generally. On momentum and physiology and the need to build. He may not have used exactly those words but the appreciation was absolutely there. Electrifying – but what a dumbo I was for assuming this kid lacked strategic intelligence). Maybe twenty minutes in and we were ripe for a gear-change.

Before the session I had no real idea whether we'd be able to do bat-skills stuff. Now I knew we could. But we'd need to start with big balls – footballs – and continue to judge and re-calibrate.

I had two pitches set up; the stumps were maybe irrelevant (depending) but they are visual and therefore maybe something of a focal point. I asked the kids (yes!) if they could help me out again by getting into four 'mini-teams', facing each other, behind the wickets. (Teachers often instinctively intervene here and start designating Jo to that group and Sara to that one, instead of letting the kids sort this - by calculation and agreement. Of course this can take time but it's surely better to get the children to try to do the simple maths and less simple communication *if possible* - at least for a few moments? Whatever: minor, perhaps).

Moving on, I had to point out that those yellow pole-things were what we in cricket call wickets. With the kids soon gathered – mostly, predictably, by the guiding hand of teachers in this case - I knew that this configuration would mean that there would only be two or three children in each mini-queue, meaning lots of activity, even if we did relay-type movements. I did then demonstrate

taking the ball across, on the floor, with lots of little touches.

So dribbling, with the ball. Sounds easy but not necessarily, eh? (Watch Primary School kids up to about Years 5 and 6 – 9 or 10-ish – and you will see that many will not instinctively grab hold of the bat and do this comfortably).

As they start, I am probably saying

why are we doing this, then, friends? I think we are trying to find a way that's comfortable – a way of holding this bat and maybe controlling this ball... with lots of little touches. But hey; let's have lots of goes and see if we can work this out.

'Sporty teachers' at this point often intervene to tell Jo or Sara to hold it with two hands, to get their strong hand below their weaker one. I prefer to let it go, at least for a while, whilst maybe gently asking a question or two...

How do we make this work? How do we make it feel right?

I make sure these kids get a few fumbles through this before a) changing the ball for a slightly smaller one – the orange All Stars balls, for those in the know - and b) asking the group how many hands they need on the bat. Having watched carefully and weighed-up what might be appropriate I then added in some hoops, on the floor, as 'roundabouts' which the children now have to go around. Again

lots of little touches... and now you're really going to need to get those two hands on the bat... and try to get them comfortable.

Now there's plainly a higher degree of challenge, and of coordination required. Asking quite a lot, of some of the group – I knew that. But the quality of effort and concentration and healthy intensity has also gone up, in a way that is patently positive. Meanwhile I'm offering more encouragement:

wow, earthlings, this is ridiculously good. I don't think I'm supposed to be giving you marks out of ten any more but I reckon this is 28, no 56 out of 10! Ridiculous! Look at you, A, if you get any better I'm gonna have to escort you to the police station!

Yes, it is *that daft*. But I swear we're all loving it, now.

I introduce a 'spot' – a flat, circular marker, to the centre of our pitches. I say

Friends it's time to do some booming. So forget the roundabouts. We're going to dribble the ball – weird word, what's all that about? – to the centre spot... and then hit it, strike it, to try and make it hit the wickets at the far end.

Look I know you don't have to have a score, to make a game, right? But how many points do you think we should give ourselves, if we hit?

Z says *'two!'*

*Ok brill. If we hit, we get two points for our team. Now if we can, we're going to try to stop the ball on that spot in the middle, with the bat, not our hands or our feet – **if we can** – and then hit. Okay? Let's have a go!*

Again the gentle upskilling thing is accepted by the kids. They are really trying. It's lovely to watch. Teachers supporting. Children battling nobly or fiddling hard. After a few minutes I make the point that nobody can get hurt here, so we can **enjoy hitting hard** – hard but straight if we can. I think I may have demonstrated how a sideways stance with the ball in the middle of my feet – *so look, under my head* – feels comfy to me. But I certainly didn't use the word stance, or actually even hit a ball. Want *them* to do that; them to find a way that works.

Couple more minutes and we forget going to the centre. We just move away from our wickets a little then boom the ball all the way down the pitch. X suggests that's *godda be worth ten points*, for a hit, so ten points it is. And I'm encouraging everybody to

Un-leaaash the beee-eassstt!!

We are probably towards 40 minutes in to this now. As he walked out, one of the teachers had said

This could go one of two ways, Rick. Don't worry if we don't get past 20 mins.

The pitch-length ball-striking is fine, but I want these kids to finish off with the properly satisfyingly wallop of a ball from a tee.

Absolute booming.

It's certainly something of a cliché, but the activity I do always refer to as The Boomathon is both popular and truly, deeply enjoyable, for most children. Partly because **they can all do it.** We take it in turns to blast a ball off a plastic tee; generally about four batters, with fielders out there receiving/catching/collecting the balls. Absolute freedom to give it a right good clout. Needs a little supervision, to keep folks safe (and ensure violence-free sharing) but if the hitting is successfully shared around and the fielders dissuaded from diving on top of each other too wildly, it flies. I use it to offer that much-needed liberation as well as to coach medium-sophisticated ideas around how 'taking turns' can make a game work.

In this case – with these nine 'misfits' – it was a delightful, nay sumptuous and appropriate way to finish our session. We stayed with the All Stars balls (decent grapefruit-sized) and the kids walloped with gusto, sometimes connecting, sometimes not. In this small group they got lots of chances to hit; so lots of success. It's not exaggerating too wildly to say there was a kind of ecstasy in the air.

*

I hope this chapter conveys something of the mood of this session. It feels a tad unhelpful to omit names, personalities, individual achievements. The essence of its colour – and it was colourful – was something to do with people being recognized, brought on, supported, valued for who they were and are. I don't mean this to be about me, I really don't. I know there are zillions of sports teachers and coaches from many other sports doing equivalent or better work than I ever could, in schools and in clubs all over. It's happening daily – thank god. This is just another ode to the uplifting and transforming power of sport.

Nine extraordinary children had a fantastic 50 minutes or so. They listened, moved, created, swelled, boomed, behaved... and I promise it was remarkable. So much so that I felt compelled to add it in to this wee tome, rather belatedly.

The one teacher that I recognized as he came out with this group said it was brilliant as he thanked me and took the children back in. Oh, and by the way, having been politely challenged by a grateful and rather humbled coach *to do that lining up thing*, the Magnificent Nine followed their five teachers in - beautifully and quietly.

EIGHTEEN - THE (BEST TAKE CARE HOW WE USE THIS WORD) MERCURIAL.

If you were to ask me what the most difficult thing in cricket was I might say facing bowling that's too quick for you. That's both scary and bewildering in a way that can be genuinely intimidating. If you can't move your body parts – hands, arms, torso, head – sharply to play the ball how you need to then your physical safety, as well as your contribution with the bat, is in peril. (There's no way I could cope with quick bowling even at club level now: reactions are gone).

However if we were to talk more about skills than dangers then we'd take a journey into more pleasing and less menacing territory: leg-spin. Leg-spin is magbloodynificent and tricky and yes, mercurial. It's for Beautiful Maniacs. Van Gogh, Kurt Cobain, Duncan McKenzie, Marcel Duchamp and Björk were all/are all leg-spinners.

For cricket virgins let me offer a brief description: as always things are contingent upon *what kind of bowler/ batter* is in play, so let's make clear the assumption that a right-hander is bowling to a right-hander. Leg-spin then is the art – and I think that word is appropriate – of spinning or turning the ball off the pitch *away* from the batter's chest. (The batter stands sideways-on, yes? In this case left foot closest to the bowler.) The word spin implies that the ball is not moving quickly; so we're talking relatively slow bowling, here.

But why so difficult? Perhaps I should add that it's *difficult to be consistent.* Why so? Because – probably – the movements are 'wristier' and more extravagant than the major alternative – off-spin. Leg-spinners tend to cock their wrists before they turn their arm over to deliver. They then flick their wrists and/or fingers anti-clockwise to impart spin. *Generally,* leg-spin bowlers can get more spin than 'offies', by using the third finger of the bowling hand to grip and rotate the seam of the ball. The greater the wrist and finger action, the more revolutions will be imparted onto the ball. Pitch quality is massive in cricket – that's why all that preamble and psychobollocks pre-game[44] - because it will determine amount of spin and bounce.

Bowling coaches might now be bawling about the contribution of hips and thrust but there is enough truth in the above to offer a meaningful way in to this. It is by nature an ambitious series of movements; mysterious and often deliberately deceptive. Not everybody who bowls leg-spin makes it seem radical; not everyone

---

[44] The toss: when captains, having appraised the pitch, decide what it's 'likely to do'. Then choose, if they can, whether it would be advantageous to bat or bowl.

'turns it miles'. But it is one of the quiet glories of cricket because of those heady possibilities.

*

At the elite level bowlers need – buzzword alert – 'variations', to survive. (That is, they have to be able to keep batters guessing, by having a roster of different deliveries). Batters, to counter, look to *read* – i.e predict – those deliveries. If the batsman plays and misses, you will often hear the commentators say something like *"oof. (S)he didn't pick it!"* Meaning (s)he was unable to discern (from the bowler's body-movements and wrist/finger action, in particular) what kind of ball was coming down the track. To be clear, top, top players will be looking to read every delivery: they know it gives them a significantly greater chance of playing the ball safely and/or with aggression should they choose.

That whole mind-games ball-game adds a delicious extra level to proceedings. Because leg-spinners by definition are slow bowlers, this contest is more even, in this respect, than with 'quicks'. One example: the degree to which the bowler's hand has been turned – and therefore the amount of the back of the hand visible to the batter at release – may be key to reading the googly. (Eek. A googly is a theoretically leg-spin delivery which actually turns the other way). And this may be readable, in a leg-spinner's action. Possibly.

There is, as you can see, no 'in short' here but in short leg-spin is the source of particular, often left-field drama. It's profoundly important to the game of cricket because of its unpredictability and yes, the mysteries and challenges around execution and response. Rich territory. Despite my initial list, leg-spinners are Fauves, maybe, or Abstract-Expressionists. They gamble and they contort: colourfully.

*

Shane Warne bowled what became known as the 'ball of the century' to Mike Gatting. If I describe it as an orthodox leg-spin delivery – i.e spinning away from the right-handed former England skipper – that underappreciates it somewhat. The ball spat a mile across him and clattered his off stump, with Gatts petrified in bewilderment. It was the stocky, habitually lary Australian's first ball in Test cricket. He finished with 708 Test wickets.

If a decent leg-spin delivery moves about four inches, this lurched about four or five times that distance. Unplayable, is the word. Warne had ripped a phenomenal amount of revolutions into the ball by snapping that wrist and the seam of the ball had bitten into the ground. It was one of the most shocking and exhilarating moments in the history of cricket. It was Jackson Pollock, action painting *and* pissing into the fireplace at the same time.[45]

*

---

[45] There is a story that the wildish, alcoholic American Abstract Expressionist did a contemptuous wee-wee into the fireplace at some gallery view. With arty-folks watching.

In those aforementioned broader revolutions within the game, currently, one of the most satisfying might be the increase in value of the leg-spinner. This applies in particular in regard to short-format cricket, where the likes of Adil Rashid and Rashid Khan are both World Stars and Extremely Hot Properties. The former, after years of being trivialized because of that alleged tendency towards inconsistency – and maybe we best not rule out some degree of racism? - has blossomed into sumptuous maturity. There is even meaningful talk of him being recalled to the England Test team, where previously his impacts had been considered too fickle, too unreliable. Khan is arguably the most desirable commodity in T20 cricket, world-wide, for his bowling smarts, essentially.

Given that cricket manages to seem both fixated on T20 *and* absolutely clear that Tests are the blue-riband configuration, it's may be hard for a stellar player to know where to concentrate his energies: except money. (Important note: currently there's still no major money available for women – although this is an *evolving situation*. This is why I exclude them here). Rashid, in the knowledge that England Cricket were unconvinced of his value as a Test player *and* fully aware of his likely value in better-remunerated 50 Over and T20 formats, pulled out of County Championship cricket (red ball, four day), for Yorks. It was controversial but made complete sense - particularly as he had suffered injury. He has since become an outstanding, bold, reliable bowler; a short-format fixture for England but strangely overlooked by the mighty, cash-rich IPL.

Rashid Khan, on the other hand is featuring at T20 tourneys all over. His ability to get wickets and/or keep the run-rate down being a huge bonus to his franchise-of-the-month. (Again that sounds cynical. Have no issue with Khan's cashing-in: he's special and it's kindof wonderfully counter-intuitive that his cool but strident artistry is getting so-o rewarded by such a shamelessly financially-driven enterprise. There's both a soul to what he does and a circus around it).

The raison-d'etre for leg-spin bowlers has always been to trick, confuse, mystify. Remember they haven't got the blessing that is pace: batters are being befuddled, ideally by guile and deception, loop and spin. And this theatre extends out, intoxicatingly for us viewers, beyond merely what is bowled. Batters' minds are being shredded by the concealment and illusion around those deadly variations.

NINETEEN – OFF-SPIN.

"45 degrees. Turn the key. It's easy". Some of the things I've heard, said, thought, in relation to off-spin. The obvious things – or the ones that 'crop up instinctively'.

Off-spin has always struck me as relatively straightforward to achieve but this is not, of course, to say that the likes of Graeme Swann or Nathan Lyon are or have been doing something intrinsically less challenging or less skilled than Rashid Khan. (Hmmm. Know what? Part of me thinks they may be. But that's ridiculous – and will divide the cricketing universe - so let's close this para out with something uncontentious). Off-spin, often known as finger spin, is the art based around turning the ball *in* – assuming the bowler is right-handed - towards a right-handed batter.

Guessing 80 percent of you reading that know this. Meaning twenty-odd don't. For the benefit of that twenty let me unpick, a little, my first three sentences.

Forty-five five degrees, because many in the game believe sending the ball down there, spinning, *with the seam at forty-five degrees to the vertical,* tilted towards the batter, is important. I remember vividly attending a coach workshop led by Robert Croft, the former

Glamorgan and England player, in which he stressed this repeatedly. Why? Because if you impart clockwise revs on the ball, by 'turning the key', or mimicking that (clockwise) movement and set the ball off with the seam at forty-five degrees, then that seam is likely to grip, on landing and kick on and in. If you exacerbate the revolutions on the ball by flicking or driving that action, with your first finger against the seam, then you may really be in business.

This sounds relatively complicated and maybe it is. But letting the ball slide out, whilst turning that key, and even doing it repeatedly and accurately, is achievable. Wonderfully, the same ensuing magic, trauma and/or marginal gains exist at every level of the game; what changes is the quality and consistency of execution.

Great off-spinners need guile and variety every bit as much as their wrist-spinning counterparts. (Possibly even more so, given that few 'offies' turn the ball a significant distance, or sufficiently to beat or seriously discomfort the batter by spin alone). They also need to get into the heads of their opponents.

Some of this is simply verbals, or body-language; trying to generate tension or fuel anger or distraction in the batter. Constant, stifled appealing or knowing looks as the ball is marginally miscued, or the batsman withdraws from the shot. Registering your animal presence. Following through with deliberately irritating, faux expectation.

Inevitably, it's the more cultured stuff, the less 'positive', obvious or even odious contributions from the spinner that tends to feed the need of Serious Cricket People for subtlety and that critical appreciation for slowness.

Cricket, particularly Test and County Championship, or equivalent, is about challenges over time. Patience, thought and rigour become as valuable as flair and dynamism - quite possibly uniquely so, in a game that does feature so much flair and dynamism. Maybe cricket's capacity for gathering afficionados of a particular sort and its alleged snobbery and impenetrability to some *centres* around the occurrence and quality of this near-stasis. It's a place where some can see, feel, recognize a whirlwind brewing and others just see a vacuum where they think sport should be. This kind of cricket ver-ry rarely bores me but I can see why some struggle: we in cricket need to see why they do.

*

The off-spinning contribution to the contest is frequently subtle. It's about playing the long game, providing minor shifts in rhythm, line, length, degree of 'air'. It's about loop and a few mph either way. Or metronomic persistence then a wee change. The loveliness – often unhurried - is different. The bowler is probing for frustrations yet un-born or marking a holding-pattern. Success, much less glory, can seem a distant prospect but that's okay when the spinner is thinking in sequences more than slam-dunks.

*

I watched current Australian spin-king Nathan Lyon offer another web masterclass before writing this. He's one of those guys who seems to have something of the Everyman about him: this includes his bowling. Sometimes it's not clear where he gets this proud, ongoing international career from. I mean, what's he actually doing with the ball? It feels like not that much.

Maybe my view of this is more twisted than I thought? Best bullet-point some feelings.

- He's Australian, and he does have his moments of really crass Oz Machismo.
- The nickname thing – Garry. *Yawns*. Harmless but empty #bantz? Still – bit irritating.
- His bowling. Doesn't turn it much. How come all the caps and all the wickets?
- To be fair, he seems completely unfashionable and uninterested in image. Which is good.
- So… how does he get to be 'world class?' Best see what he's got to say for himself.

Unsurprisingly, Lyon is no master of the master class. He's too modest, too un-showy, for that. But in talking about his work – his off-spin – the layers peel away a little and we get what we nearly always get; a top player revealed as a tremendously committed professional. A man dedicated to understanding and improving his art. Integrity and sporting intelligence beyond our expectation.

I hadn't thought enough about how Lyon does his thing. Via those google-found videos I learned specifically that he's much more interested and even focused on getting 'overspin – i.e. extra bounce – to trouble his opponent than gaining lateral or conventional spin. (Stupid of me, quite possibly. Maybe I'm so sucked in to the romantic notion of the ball lurching sideways that I failed to see the value of the other tricks).

Lyon shared generously and fully (as bowlers tend to do) his description of how he sets the seam vertically and rolls fingers up and over the back of the ball to impart that top-spin. This is his 'stock ball', because it can draw an error: on flat pitches, there may be no lateral movement available to spinners but bounce may vary or *be encouraged* to vary. He will of course look to mix things up, by throwing in the 45 degrees notion, changing pace and his position around the crease... but Garry's all about loop and over-spin or top-spin. And I under-estimated his skill around that.

*

I never wanted to be a spin bowler – until now, perhaps, with the pace option a distant memory. (Currently I'm seriously considering a late flowering as a leggie: couple of issues. One, broke my hand sledging two years ago[46] and can't turn it over like I used to. Two, I still love running in, even if it's embarrassing to my kids and my team-mates).

*

---

[46] True. Dog – our dog - chased me down the village slope and grabbed at my hand. (Lols). And ouch.

May refrain from putting a date on this but some of my early sporting memories are of Derek Underwood. We didn't exactly gather round the box when England were playing cricket – Christ Almighty we did when the footie was on! – but I remember Derek, un-fussily wheeling in, on a classically grainy telly. Grandma Sarah of Station Road with that thin voice may have been there, peering up from her needlework. (Yes really. Another age, one where cricket was visible but as yet not entirely compelling, to me. By contrast I recall the sharpness in Grandma's eye and her tribal fixation on the Roses Match).

Underwood's bowling fairly quickly in those memories; skittling half the universe. Don't remember all that much spin, to be honest but that could be erroneous. Loop and maybe a rhythm that hurried people, somehow? He was a menace, as were uncovered pitches – both wonderfully so - but maybe that's another book.

*

Let's zip forward to the present – or the moment of writing, at least. How refreshing to be able to report that Sophie Ecclestone (of England) may be the most dominant off-spinning force in world cricket: she really may. Meanwhile two male spinners are plying their trade together, also for England, in Sri Lanka, with the Indian Test Series Spin-fest looming nicely. Another one is still hassling the ECB and the twittersphere, I think to re-centralise himself in the national conversation: at least in cricket.

Just me, or is Graeme Swann The Man Who Tries Too Hard? Not on the pitch, where his bowling contribution was often a revelation, but off it, where his tinny chumminess and rock-star wannabee-ness are keeping him in the frame for either an England Spin Consultancy or a Reality TV Something.

Swanny was a truly threatening offie with a flow and dynamism that made him top-level watchable as well as essential to the team. He was without question world-class. Weird though, that we sense that this means he thinks he's somehow entitled to a role in coaching the current squad. What is that thing whereby folks don't get the difference between playing and coaching? Ego? For sure. Swann's exasperation at his 'exclusion' is fascinating.

TWENTY – BANTER, BRILLIANCE & GENEROSITY: THE COMPANY OF MEN.

Something unbeatable but true. Or, o-kaaay may be beatable so maybe not true. But who cares, when it's a great story? *Language alert*.

As a youff and youngish man I played football. Half-decently. I was gifted the honour – and yes I do mean that – of being First Team Captain at Healing Royal British Legion Sunday Football Club,[47] aged 21-ish, ahead of ridicu-stalwarts like Graham Alyson and John Smith. I was starting to boss games a little, from centre-midfield but it was a gamble, one I relished then and still appreciate deeply today. Better men than me had stood aside to encourage this Walton Boy to grow and even to lead.

I also signed, after some thought and a little persuasion, for Immingham Town, who were playing a level up, on Saturday afternoons. (I remember playing against David Nish, ex- Leicester and Derby County, early

---

[47] Nope. I haven't made up that name. Played in the Grimsby Sunday League. Magic. Tough. *Developmental* and sometimes just mental.

doors, in a cup match: I had seen him play brilliantly for England years before. I ghosted past him into the box to score our second goal with a simple header – great ball from Stuart Gray, the former Grimsby Town centre-back).

Healing were my team, though: that ground was where we grew up, in so many ways. Two of my brothers were also playing for the village, when not at college and my dad had played before us. We played alongside Mooney brothers, Pauls and Winships: it was magnificently clannish in the way most recreational sport is. Living next door to our house and yet closer to the hallowed ground, club icon Cliff Winship was mentor and Football Dad to all of us, especially after our father succumbed to heart attack while three of us were still at school.

I was youngish and maybe not tough enough to settle, or feel a real part of the Immingham set-up. More my fault than theirs. There were some good guys but I just didn't have the love for the club that I had for our village side. I eased away, having got a rare injury and without doing myself justice.

The standard at Immingham was a tad higher than the Sunday footie: there was more bite to training and to matches. This didn't mean there weren't laughs. There was an Assistant Manager at the club who was the backroom comedian and sometime cheerleader. The Manager, a slightly dour fella, often let this guy do the team-talks. On one occasion, now legendary, he let rip with the most incredible tirade of what used to be called foul language – is it still? Haven't heard that phrase for aeons? – that has ever echoed round a changing-room.

It was remarkable in several respects: chiefly, because somehow it wasn't abusive of anybody. It wasn't, in essence malicious, or especially impassioned. It *was, definitely* partly for the laughs but somehow fell short of being mere panto. It was an absolute torrent of meaningless fucks.

Stugger, you're the fucking leader, today – you always fucking are. Get these fuckers going. Get the ball from the keeper and get it into midfuckingfield. Warvy – stay wide. That fucking left-back is about as much use as the Pope's bollocks. You'll annihilate the fucker. Ricky, we've got to get you on the fucking ball, pal. So play inbefuckingtweeeen. Get fucking dancing. Flick a few one-fucking-twos in to fucking Martyn. The fucker can't run but he'll give you it back. Fucking express yourself, son…

Barry Tong(?) and Phil Carrington had slipped behind him and were counting the effs. Carro' called it at 72. Seventy fu-cking two! Weirdly, honestly, I remember it more as natural flow than performance: it *wasn't* being camped-up, for laughs. The bloke talked like that, in the company of men.

*

The bloke who got me to sign for Immingham was Terry Paul. He was one of two brothers who played for

Healing. Terry was quietish and wore glasses, like his brother, Ginge (or Ginger, or Keith) but they were as fascinatingly different as their specs. (Terry had the subtle-but-shiny jobs of a clerk or middle-manager; Keith the regulation black plastic NHS issue that now has a strangely cool equivalent amongst fashionistas or media-types). They both played full-back and were both senior players – i.e. 'oldish', longstanding, loved – during my years in the side.

Ginger was a warrior and a good player; tough but also could pass. Needed a fag before the match and at half-time, when *we did*, incidentally, suck on chunks of orange and occasionally, when the North Sea gale was really bitter, sup sweet tea from the feeblest of plastic cups. There were times when it was painful magic – not that this seemed to bother Ginger Paul. Cases of hypothermia were not uncommon but not even the Mongolian blasts could penetrate his steadfast, tobacco-rich armour.

Terry had been club secretary at Immingham, I think and being both softly-spoken and yes, bespectacled, struck me - still punky and brewing existential, anti-capitalist angst - as something of an office wallah; a deeply likable one, I should say. (Remain unclear on this and disinclined, currently, to commit to further research... but solicitor is possible).

Our Unlikely Hero was strongly-built but neither dynamically robust in the way that his quietly tigerish brother was, nor as cute with his feet. In fact, cruel haplessness sometimes singled him out. We had a standing joke about his unerring ability to find a spot thirty yards off the field of play when searching for that drilled, left-foot pass down the line towards our vainly galloping winger.

(In his defence we did all get plenty of bobbles on that pitch but Terry's studied look up and forward and his compellingly loud call, before the inevitable 45 degree slice, became part of the folklore of the club. I will never forget Cliff doing wonderfully good-natured impressions of Bewildered Terry... or Cursing the Wind Terry, or Terry Who Can't Be-lieeeeve That Bloody Divot - Again).

But there is more. One particular Sunday morning; home match. Kick-off 10.45 so ace but habitually tardy striker Bernie Mooney just arriving in a screech of brakes as the occasionally-visible Grimsby Dock Tower struck 10.50. Conditions not at issue from what I recall but Terry was already struggling. Half eleven we take our oranges and he is still chuntering about his left foot not feeling great; cue, obviously, the jokes about Terry's Left Foot. He sits by the touchline as we mither about the ref or their bustling midfielder. Then a strange moment of exclamation and, typically, self-deprecation as Terry holds up the comb just removed from inside his boot.

I've played the whole flippin' half with a comb inside me boot!

*

So much for the laughs, which have been many and life-enhancing, in and around football, cricket and rugby changing-rooms. (Was an assistant coach to top fella Pete Williams, at Haverfordwest RFC, briefly, when my son was playing at junior level. Fabulous: taught me a lot). But whilst acknowledging and even championing the essential wit at the core of the enjoyment of team sport, I want to bludgeon further, get deeper. Because the power of this thing – abstract though it is – *makes people,* yes? Zillions of us take this for fact and yet can we ever really say how or why?

I learned early that some folks can barely write but stick 'em on a footie/cricket/rugby pitch – or even in a dressing-room – and their smarts, their canniness, the brilliance of their skills or humour can light up the company. They become something wholly bigger and more valuable. They *register* - 'ordinary' guys and gals. Sometimes it's their capacity for waggishness, sometimes the hugeness, loyalty and generosity of their hearts. Occasionally, their souls just sing, quietly, through the act of playing, as though liberated from some prevailing restraining-order. I have known plenty of young lads or young men who would learn or accept twenty years after the event that football was both their escape into fullness and their therapy.

Surely the *actual movement* plays a part in this? Watching young kids in my cricket sessions it strikes me so often that **just moving** sets them off into some fabulous, rich, personal adventure. I've barely offered anything – other than an invitation to jog together, or pass a ball around – and the joy is immediately palpable. Something starts, or fires up. Throw in the hustle and the whir of a match, with comrades, and a whole new level of the human condition releases itself. I don't fixate on competitive sport, by any means but I do froth quite happily when it comes to teams. They are a wonder of life.

Let me do that urgent bullet-pointing thing again; this time to flush out some of the Best Things I Ever Did (which relate to sport). Then maybe you do the same. Simply as an Ode to Activity: from all of us.

- Played football for and then captained Healing Royal British Legion Sunday Football Club. Often hung-over; always, despite my youth, conscious of the greatness of the blokes around me. (Half the team, including my impressionable self, would go out and drink lots of pints of beer on the Sat'dee Night. Or even go clubbing, which meant shorts, probably; large bacardi and coke times several (after the beers) and a bop to Depeche Mode. Jesus). I often reflect on how I might be *now* if I drank the same volume: how able to contemplate pret-ty competitive sport, on a 10.45a.m. start?
- There was one famous occasion – actually of course it wasn't but my god it was noteworthy to the point of biblical in its beery imprint. Eldest brother's 21st coincided with his exit towards Calibloodyfornia, for a year at USC.[48] We had a monster party in our back garden: whole team invited. Only 'Spenny', the leggy but dynamic and versatile lad from The Willows dipped out. (Fireman: on shift). Some of the toughest men in Grimsby were begging to come

---

[48] Think he'd won a journalism scholarship-thing.

off at half-time. Our dependable stopper, John Smith, played most of the 90 minutes without heading the ball. At centre-back. In a Sunday League fixture. That thing you hear about teams 'surviving'... well it was that. We won one-nil, with Spenny scoring the winner.

- Went to Canada. Played football (indoors, mid-winter) for Italia, one of two soccer teams from the Italian Community of Thunder Bay. Wonderful madness - a book all on its own. Treated like a celebrity, along with my bro' T Whitley Esq, because we were the best players around: 'cos they were, yaknow, Canadians. Toured into Minnesota briefly, with Thunder Bay All Stars, where I may have got MVP of the tournament... but the memory is yaknow, blurred.

- Moved permanently to Pembs, aged about 22, having done the summer job thing there previously. Signed for Solva Athletic Football Club, where again the privileges and the comradeship were joyous and humbling. I was, at one time, the only bloke not born within about a three mile radius, in the team. It will mean nothing to most of you but believe me the fact that I later followed Nobby Howells as club captain (and as an outsider) is my Olympic gold. My years in Ronnie Beynon's/ Matthew Raggett's/Sion Young's/Tony Walsh's/Paul Adams's Solva side were magnificent and rich and bloody daft in a way that defies translation – except of course to or by those who have their own, splendiferous equivalent. And many do.

- Aged about 45, I took my son to Haverfordwest Cricket Club, having been informed by him that "some of the boys were going". I threw the ball back six times, then began coaching... and then learning to coach cricket. I volunteered for several years before a job came up with Cricket Wales... and lo and behold.

*

I wanted to write about Graham Everett – left-back - for his relentless honesty and Bernie Mooney, for his courage, heart and Roy-of-the-Rovers-like 'leading of the line'. Our line. But enough. More of that one day, perhaps. For now I am reminding myself that the genius of these guys is this: they made it impossible and unthinkable to be anything other than a believer in the value of everybody. Their stories are as marvellous and true as any. Stick me back in that dressing-room with them, all of them - the donkeys, jesters, hooligans, Brexiters and the fuckers who can't write or think. Stick 'em in my team and I will see, feel and help them shine. And they will do the same for me.

TWENTY-ONE – "WHERE YOU FROM, ANYWAY?"

Weirdly, I can't remember the match – could have been West Brom at The Hawthorns. Was certainly a big Town occasion, an away-day. I was about fifteen.

We'd gone to support the Mighty Mariners, in a cup game. I know I should remember which one but just can't quite grasp that: there were quite a few. We're on the terraces with that testosterone load that you get when you're on foreign territory but you came in good numbers. You're kinda pathetically proud that you've surprised the opposition support. They think you're lower-league scumbags but you turn up in thousands and do that "ooooooaahhhh" with ironic but bitter animosity when the stadium announcer asks that "the Grimsby Town fans please move forward and down the terrace to allow those queueing at the back of the stand to enter safely". It's edgy; it often was, in the seventies.

*

I say hello to a lad I know from school. He's a tall one, with forearms but was always known as a fraudulent tough-guy. He has a denim jacket on and a Town scarf tied around his wrist. His mate, whom I don't know, is looking agitated and sounding confrontational. There are opposition fans pressed against the fence ten yards to our left, with police dotted along that line. Either side of that insubstantial barrier there are guys who want to scrap and this young bloke – a weasly-looking youth but the sort who might get involved – is constantly looking and gesturing towards the home fans.

I clearly remember him saying he "*really* wanted a fight, tonight". There was a pent-up rage going-on, which was both convincingly evil and pitiful. He was looking directly at me, as I was talking briefly to our mutual acquaintance. Reading my face, which was plainly saying something like "who *is* this arsehole?" he lurched towards me saying "you Grimsby, or what? Who are you?" The big fella cheerfully stopped him (before he started) by confirming that I was indeed 'Grimsby' but this sticks shockingly clearly in the memory because this pale distracted youff *really was* ready to start smackin' away at a fellow Town fan, in the midst of thousands of fellow Town fans, who had travelled a hundred and odd miles to support their hometown club. But football did that, back then. Maybe it still does today?

*

A further story about football and violence – sadly it did accompany, or the threat or possibility for violence did accompany almost every visit to a football ground we made, between about 1970 and 1980-odd. Fortunately, for some of that period I was simply too young to get personally targeted but the smell of 'aggro' was always close at hand. You kept your wits about you, suspecting, fearing or watching out.

I have a vivid recollection of stepping away from Geordie voices, on the way in to Blundell Park, as a kid. Turned out, as they passed that they were good-natured fifty-year-old blokes, genuinely and cheerily exchanging banter with local fans. That went on for a couple of hundred yards before we pointed them towards the Away Supporters End. I had completely traduced them: it felt weird but you had to be aware of who was around you.

The tale that follows is a classic in the post-modern sense: there are things which are really hard to describe and to know. I am both unable to confirm certain (possibly live) issues of race and sexual identity and a bit frightened of delivering an offensive travesty. I have tried to clarify through contact some of the concerns but failed to do so. Yet because it remains a powerful memory this now fraught story is something I want to relate. I know what happened but can only speculate on some of the causes. Here goes.

*

My eldest brother was in the same school year as Terry Donovan, who played for Town and later Aston Villa. We all knew Terry well; he was a good lad and an exceptional player, gaining England caps at youth level and later two (I think) caps for the Republic of Ireland. Our Chris played alongside him at school and county level and I played a single game alongside them both, for our school First Eleven, when I was a Fourth Year. (Was chuffed to gain that relatively rare privilege. Remember to this moment Mike Hetherington, our PE Teacher telling me he thought I deserved the experience because of my "outstanding football brain"). Terry was a threat, that day: it was always purely a matter of time before he turned pro'.

As a family, we went to see Terry play for Grimsby Town, at Man City, in the League Cup. I have a strong feeling it was Terry's debut but this was probably 1979 so forgive me if I get that wrong: the fact that my mother came with us suggests it was an occasion.

Town was the sort of club that had a properly ardent fan-base but not that many... yet when Big Glamorous Cup Ties came along, thousands would go. (Soonish, I'm going to re-count a tale of a trip to Anfield, in which between six and seven thousand Town fans descended on Liverpool. For this trip to Maine Road - midweek, League Cup not FA Cup - I reckon it was probably 2-3,000).

So a night match, on Moss Side. Poignant for us, because our beloved Dad – born Macclesfield, City through and through – was already comparing notes with Tony Book on the sky-blue bench in heaven. Not much time for sentiment, as it turned out; this was to be pretty much the scariest night of my life.

*

Going *into* the ground was frightening enough. Peak Football Hooligan Era: dodgy alleys and deep dark shadows. Streets busy and then not. Town fans in groups, most of us scrambling around trying find the Away Supporters entrances. At the time, us fairly streetwise guys knew that some opposition fans would be looking for opportunities: some of our lot would take a kicking. Sometimes that kicking was until you were unconscious. I carried that fear in, alongside the notion that my mother was at my elbow: she wouldn't understand or know the signs.

My eldest brother had brought a mate, Mark, a lovely, thoughtful bloke who may have been a fellow student at Oxford University. (Before you go jumping to conclusions, a couple of facts. Chris was educated in the state system – we all were. He got into Oriel College, Oxford because he was well capable and because he was a bloody outstanding sportsman. He ultimately got 'blues' for football – three, I think - and possibly a half-blue(?) for golf. Oh - and Chris is straight).

I barely knew Mark, so would not presume to know how he identifies in any sense, then or now. But it feels not inappropriate, given events, to note that his skin was of a slightly darker pigment than mine (which is white – I would identify as white British) and that *I suspect* that this was a factor in that which transpired, post-game. I can be clearer that before the match, we were turned away from a Manchester pub when *something about Mark* – who was wearing an Anti-Nazi League badge – offended the bouncer at the door.

Still remember the wry smile from our friend and the bouncer's miserable awkwardness. A poor start.

*

Like lots of football grounds, Maine Road was in a properly working-class area. Like Blundell Park,[49] it had alleys (we called them snickets) leading between the stark, barely-lit streets or houses. As we walked in, and felt the presence of the City fans – some in mobs, some perfectly harmless – we stayed close and, where possible, stayed close to significant bundles of Grimsby supporters. It was impossible, I think, to avoid the alleys entirely but we did what we could to stay out. At one point my mum – then about 40 - leant in to say "Crikey. You can really feel the atmosphere, can't you?" You could.

We got in okay and Town acquitted themselves well enough. As always, the floodlights made it seem magical: as always, there were missiles being thrown, probably in both directions but we felt far enough away from the coins and the darts to relax, during play. It wasn't a classic night but there were some wonderful choruses of "Maaaaarrrin-nnerss" and Terry went well enough.

Town were losing 2-0 when Chris suggested we leave a bit early: I knew immediately it was madness. We would be exposed, picked off. I could hardly say exactly that in

---

[49] Home of the Mighty Mariners – Grimsby Town. (Incidentally, as pub-quizzers may know, it's in Cleethorpes).

front of our mum but I did raise the argument. Chris – who I realise now has always been a tad less sensitive or streetwise than me, despite him being three years my senior – prevailed. He was right that if we could get to the main road (where our car was parked) we'd be able to escape the city way quicker than those who braved the mass exodus. He was stupid to think the risks weren't very real.

We probably left five minutes early. Not sure of any of us inhaled *at all* as we slunk through the alleys. Immediately it was obvious that there were groups out there waiting. A handful of Town fans had the same idea as we did and now and then we saw a policeman but there was no escaping the fear, nor the inevitable, genuinely terrifying denouement.[50] As we walked briskly and quietly to what we hoped were the bright lights of 'our' main road, a group of men began to follow, from the other side of the street. My mother later described how it had felt like a 'military operation', as their leader silently walked a little closer; just enough to raise the pitch of our fear a little, at first.

When he came closer still I could see he had a belt wrapped around his fist. He was wearing a cream or whitish wooly jumper – it was cold, that night – but no City scarf or other identification. (We heard from other fans when we got home that they had been attacked by *United* fans that evening – go figure – but that, at the

---

[50] In a recent conversation with my bro' Chris, he said this night was 'a million miles less scary' than a Tottenham/Utd game he attended, around this time. Jesus. It was petrifying enough.

time, was not unthinkable). Then there was a noise and a scuffle behind us.

As I looked around to see two Town supporters on the ground, twenty yards back, being kicked and punched, there was movement against us. Mark had been struck hard, on the side of the face by the bloke with the belt. Thank god it was something of a glancing blow because if he had hit the floor I think all of us – possibly including my mum, such was the evil in play – might have been in serious trouble. As it was, Mark fell somewhat against me and bounced back up enough to maintain a shocked but upright position. Chris turned and I think was momentarily thinking about striking back but that would have been further madness. I have no idea if any of us actually shouted "RUN" but we somehow gathered enough to leg it. I was so scared and sure we were going to get heavily, heavily smashed I did not even think to grab my mother's hand – something that shames me to this day. The four of us ran, literally, we thought, for our lives. It remains the single scariest event I can remember.

I look back and recall other things. The police, who *without question, in my view,* disappeared – that is slunk off, deliberately - when they saw the situation developing. (There were two of them close to the scene of this. They did see the gangs of fans targeting the two wee pods of Town supporters. They did disappear). The scuffs, signals, voices, as firstly the group behind us then we ourselves were attacked. There was some degree of co-ordination. Them then us. Mostly there was that fear. Darkness, hard streets, the tantalizing sense of bright yellow lights three hundred yards ahead. The endless, screaming silence before the strike. Mark being the inevitable target. My mum being almost forgotten in the scramble.

*

One more – a brief one. Town were drawn at Liverpool, in the FA Cup, in this same era. About two weeks earlier the Mariners had beaten Everton in the League Cup, much to the Toffees' embarrassment, of course. So this was both **massive** and spiky. Six or seven thousand Town fans travelled: Merseyside Police, despite being warned, were criminally underprepared. Almost uniquely, they had allowed both Everton and Liverpool to play home games on the day, with Everton kicking off early. You didn't need to be Einstein, Dixon of Dock Green or a Z-Cars afficionado to realise this was fraught with dangers but the local constabulary believed it could all be managed.

As we walked towards Stanley Park, Everton fans were lobbing half-bricks at some of our fans as they dismounted from the armada of coaches. When we got closer in to Anfield, there were plenty of young scallies strutting around, looking to create.

I saw only one minor outbreak of aggro in the ground but saw plenty to raise concerns. Because the police apparently had no inkling of the numbers of away supporters – although I do know they were warned - we were diabolically irresponsibly sent (and I do mean *instructed*) around the ground to find "other ways in".

Our little group were told to go up and into the back of The Kop, to watch the game. (This is where I saw a Town fan getting punched, for wearing a black and white scarf). The scary bit, looking back, is that dozens of us were encouraged to push hard up the back of the stairs of The Kop in order to muscle our way in to the stand proper.

It could have been a nightmare. Having reluctantly joined the scrum and somehow launched ourselves in that wave of bodies up and then over into the rearmost section of the stand and having seen the far corner-flag for a few seconds, we were cast backwards again, and out. It felt ominous to say the least.

We left and spent a tense period of time circumnavigating the stadium again before returning to the car. Apparently Town made a few friends by playing half-decent football that afternoon but lost 5-0. We barely cared. Everybody who went to football in the days when thousands stood on cruel concrete, often against concrete stanchions, will know they dodged injury, violence or full-on tragedy a time or two. We think we did that day.

TWENTY-TWO – FEMALE HEROES / HEROINES.

Shall we play that game again, where we don't allow each other to think too much, but bullet down some ideas? Okay. Here goes. Heroines, or Female Heroes, whichever suits: in the wider world, to start. Have no doubt yours will be as revealing as mine.

- Angela Carter. Spinner of wonderful fables.
- Annie Lennox. Was a particular time when she needed to be PM.
- Kate Bush. Maddish English Middle Class but also ver-ry special. (I'm thinking 'Man With the Child' and 'This Woman's Work'. And maybe 'Breathing' – though the video...)
- Kathe Kollwitz. Expressionistic conscience of the universe: incredible printmaker/artist.
- Jeanette Winterson. For her god-like brilliance. Is 'The Passion' the greatest book ever ever?
- Right now... Jacinda Ardern. No contest.
- Greta Thunberg. Also no contest.
- Reni Eddo-Lodge, Afua Hirsch, Layla F. Saad – possibly uncool to gather them together but am grateful to all for educating and challenging me so vividly, so intelligently around race, in the last few months. Fantastic, necessary contribution.

- Adrianne Lenker, woman with many names, lead vocalist with 'Big Thief', known a little and adored (who knows, maybe just in the short term[51]) by Yours F Truly for singing 'Not', which is maybe the best song of the last decade.

Now sport-wise.

- (Ver-ry early memory, I hasten to add). Mary Peters. Wonderfully infectious athlete and Proper Competitor. Remember Olympics-watching with my dad, a lifetime away - the Amateur Era thing. Her muscle: her manner. Sentimental stuff, admittedly. Makes me wonder again at how many athletes seem both engaging and lovely and articulate – winess a zillion interviews from London 2012, or almost any significant event. Does feel like an extraordinary and fascinating contrast to (certainly male, possibly female) footballers: because they're dumb... or coached towards those mind-numbing banalities?
- Marion Jones. US sprinter. Something both electrifying and weirdly calm about her presence. Can't entirely explain her impact. Later disgraced, over steroid use – so more fleeting icon than heroine.
- Denise Lewis. Stunning career as an athlete and a ground-breaking TV pundit.

---

[51] By this I simply mean that I was swept away with this particular song and that maybe there's nothing wrong with going mad for one number and then the infatuation abating? That's sometimes the way of it, yes?

- Jessica Ennis-Hill. One of those blazing talents. Watchable. Tough. Natural.
- For brevity, going to clutch cricket women together. Have particularly enjoyed the performances of and/ or heavily rooted for Heather Knight, Danni Wyatt, Anya Shrubsole, Katherine Brunt. Plus – and the thought strikes here that somebody must be writing The Book – Sarah Taylor has also been dazzlingly watchable, as both 'keeper and batter, whilst facing-down significant mental health issues. From Australia you have to tip your hat to the brilliance of Ellyse Perry and Meg Lanning, plus Megan Schutt. Also like Shabnim Ismail, of South Africa, for that haughty, fluent, pacy-thing she's got going on; that sense *she has* that she, Ismail, is the fastest on the planet.

*

Since about 2015 your correspondent has been increasingly interested in women's sports – chiefly cricket and football but also rugby. In his capacity as ECB-accredited bloggist, he has attended and written about as many women's fixtures as he has men's. Why? Who knows? We have a sporty daughter. I mix with women and girl players and have definitely been inspired by their fabulous commitment and pazzazz. I genuinely think that the low-level boom we can all sense around women's cricket is just about the most exciting and positive racket on the planet.

Most of my working life is spent going in to schools, where I swear (see above) I'm doing my best to enthuse girls for cricket. I can now do so with a whole lot more confidence that the game can offer them something. The increases in exposure, funding, quality, dynamism and professionalism in the women's elite game strike me as profoundly important in terms of right and wrong, as well as with regard to opportunity/sexual politics/ economics. At school and club, whilst there is still work to be done, the cultural sea-change is underway. It's genuinely exciting to be able to point to a meaningful career pathway in cricket, for young female talent; for the **first time ever,** that's now possible.

The intention, Covid-permitting, is to have about 60 full-time professional women cricketers funded by ECB, during 2021. (Forty players split between the eight regional centres, plus the centrally-contracted England group). This closes the gap on what the Aussies have done – and fair play to them, by the way. Australia, by far the most forward-thinking nation in terms of openings, pay and commitment, have funded their international-level women at the same rate as the men, since 2017 and have a professional player pool of about 90.

Of course there are moral imperatives landing with the England and Wales Cricket Board but plainly this is competitive sport; in those terms as well as those of beneficent conviction, it would have been unthinkable to continue to lag behind the Australian model. The progressive shift is welcome everywhere.

It's not often in life that Sports Admin feels a truly consequential and socially-relevant forum but this has felt the case, in our particular game, the last three or four years. The surge in growth, coverage and intent around this sector of cricket is thrilling and the game on the park is feeding off the new energy and resource.

*

Anya Shrubsole is bowling, in Cardiff. August Bank Holiday, 2015. Double-header; England Women v Aus at 10.30 then the blokes at 3ish. Memories are in and out. Remember being bit embarrassed and even angry that hardly anybody showed up to watch the women's game. Remember having a great view of Shrubsole's swing-thing - was immediately behind her.

She was a revelation. It's possible that she may have had the best of conditions – possible, not certain – but my main take-out from the day was that Shrubsole swung the ball a million, exhilarating miles. I knew she was a great bowler but was unprepared for this level of quality: okay, this was the first time I'd seen her live but she was the pick of all the bowlers, that day.

Shrubsole's opening spell was more productive, more threatening and *more watchable* than any bowled by Ellyse Perry, Megan Schutt or by Starc, Cummins, Stokes or Willey, later. Anya nailed 4 for 11 off her 4 overs: more wonderfully, she looked an artist, swinging it ravishingly wildly and grabbing key wickets to set up the England win. She got Lanning, already a World Star, second ball. The inswinger was going so far she was battling to keep it from zipping down leg: it was mesmerizing. Shrubsole's been a favourite ever since.

*

Anya Shrubsole's partner-in-crime/co smash-and-grabber in the England opening bowling department is Katherine Brunt. The new ball has been theirs together: it's only in the last year or so that Nat Sciver – Brunt's partner in life – and possibly the brilliant left-arm off-spinner, Sophie Ecclestone, have threatened their domination of that privilege.

The two together seem like senior bowlers in a very good way; offering different skills, being different personalities, bringing real resilience. Rarely do they let their standards slip, meaning consistency and impact over several seasons – home and away. Though there is no doubt that England have the resources and the nous to be deep into succession planning around their frontline bowlers, there is also a sense that losing both Shrubsole and Brunt at around the same time – which seems likely - will be a huge challenge.

With Brunt, anger is often close to the surface – or bullishness, perhaps? She has that Proper Quick's fire that most of us like to see in our seam bowlers: somehow she manages to combine that with the 'softest', most audacious guile. Even when in plainly incandescent Northerner mode, Brunt will often find a peach of a slower-ball, using fabulous restraint and disguise when you *just know* she wants to take the batter's head off.

The less demonstrative Shrubsole only seems to get angry with herself: even then it feels more about disappointment than actual rage. Neither, of course, get to bowl the red ball much, as there is sadly ver-ry limited Test Match Cricket for women. Both do a remarkable job of articulating the less animated white ball.

*

Some of us are both conflicted about our Englishness – raises hand, having lived in Wales for forty years – and like to see ourselves as internationalists of a sort. And therefore we *really can* enjoy brilliance from 'elsewhere' – even Australia, on times.[52]

As we have reported, Cricket Australia have led the way rather strikingly, around equality and opportunity for women and girls in cricket. England and India are following, and the nations with less available dosh are looking to find a way, not just to compete (although this must be a factor) but to **do the right thing.** Australia have made stardom possible... and they do have stars. Their enlightened approach to equality/opportunity/ funding will surely mean that they find more: they deserve to.

I'll do little more than name-check the Aussie women who have made outstanding contributions (on the pitch) to the powerful and seemingly irreversible progress going on more broadly. Those who follow the game will see little new, here, except that personal view – some of which has been from close quarters – of exceptional players at the forefront of a worthy revolution.

---

[52] Fair lump of mischief aimed at Aus, in this wee tome. *Just because* they are the rivals, right? #Bantz.

*

Ellyse Perry. Ticks a lot of boxes. Tall, athletic player who is top-of-the-range with bat and ball. Former international footballer, which figures, given that sense of a performer in utter command of an absurd range of skills. Even at the very highest level, there is sometimes the feeling that she is coasting or, perhaps particularly with the bat, that Perry is just too good for the opposition. Her record (which I won't quote, the stats generally bore me) is remarkable. Already an argument that she is the greatest female player of all time; has a likely three or four more years at her peak, injury-permitting. (This applies to her bowling more than the work with the bat, naturally). Fine, quickish bowler, incredibly important all-round player – excellent in the field - and genuine World Star.

*

Brief diversion. This bloggist has been privileged to legitimately access a few Media Centres, mainly across Wales and the South West. Given the rarity of these events[53] – and despite not getting paid to do it – he boldly committed to attending Somerset's lovely Taunton stadium to watch and write about the **Test Match** component of the Women's Ashes of 2019. (Needed the freebie, so stayed with staggeringly hospitable friends in Bristol, got the train in, daily).

---

[53] Women – contentiously – are getting ver-ry few opportunities to play Test Cricket. This seems unlikely to change, sadly.

The match was fairly heavily criticized – though not by myself - for being a bore-draw in which the Australians in particular, having the ascendancy, should have played more positively. As is the custom, certain players are 'sent up' by the Media Teams to deal with press enquiries, post the day's play. For obvious reasons, the player offered tends to be someone who has had a strong impact on the action. Perry gets the call a lot.

In mentioning the following I do note the risks around putting myself at the centre again; but these were *times I will remember* – being a fan, right?

Press Conferences proper, I simply generally skip. They are frequently almost completely meaningless, such is the need for control from the Media Team and wider governing body: The Corporation, generally, expresses itself. I'm not saying it's significantly different when players get collared - amiably enough, in my experience – for a word or two in less formal situations but personal relations *can* work differently in a huddle. In the Media Centre at Taunton, I joined the small group gathered and waiting.

Standing within four feet of Perry or Meg Lanning is not something I saw coming until it happened. (I'm at once wide-eyed and trying to be cool). Perry seems personable up close. She's certainly a professional in these situations, having been the go-to player for much of her career. I say absolutely nothing.

There's a shade more spice in the Lanning interview but it's respectfully done, on the outfield after the four days of the Test creep to a rain-affected draw. She is pushed just a little, on the lack of urgency in the game. Lanning – the captain and probably second-most famous female player on the planet (behind Perry) – is polite enough, patient enough, well-rehearsed enough. Like her team on the park, she gets the job done without much fuss.

*

Part of the gig when you cover sport is that thing about neutrality. The genuinely affable Vic Marks (who does seem a lovely guy, by the way) was conspicuously clear on this on the radio, when declaring it a "no-no" for members of the press pack to cheer for Team Z – even if it's palpably the one that they would support.

Understand that but have always felt this particular bloggist stands to one side of the legit media and therefore has a tad more freedom to be mischievous. (Not that I am, particularly). Don't expect Vic to agree, or necessarily approve of any non-mainstream writer's presence in the Media Centre(s) but providing any support is respectful enough of the scenario then... fair enough? We all have some tribal depth, do we not? Absolutely right that Proper Journalism is not partisan but okay for a semi-private punching of the Media Centre air, no? As opposed to *just pretending* to be neutral?

*

Despite the various conflictions around politics, philosophy, geography, economics and the fact of where

I've lived for forty years, I'm an England supporter, when it comes to cricket. That's not at issue because it's England *and Wales*. Football and rugby are different... and I'm not going there. Instead I want to talk about a great England captain – Heather Knight.

Knight really is something of a hero. Has that old-school England Skipper doughtiness, but has also developed her dynamism – batting-wise – to keep pace with the era. (She had seemed a conservative sort, with maybe too few tricks, lacking incendiary inclination and power. She has notably addressed these issues).

Knight can boss an entire game now, by bringing the boom in a way that didn't seem within her compass a year or so ago, *or* by playing smart, aggressive, expansive cricket through an innings. Got to rate that. Would select her in a World XI: the other England candidates would be Sciver, Ecclestone, Brunt and Shrubsole.

*

Probably the most satisfying live cricket-watch I experienced in the period 2015-19 was the Kia Super League Final at Hove, in September 2019. Knight won the game for her side, Western Storm, with a superlative, measured but also powerful 78 not out, against the grain of the event. (Danni Wyatt had threatened to take the game away from Storm with a typically energetic 73 off 42 balls, driving Southern Vipers to a strongish total of 172 for 7).

It was a beautiful day down on the Sussex coast and my first visit to Hove, which certainly rose-tinted the experience but Knight's quality throughout was authentically memorable. She appeared beatifically unflustered as Wyatt and Suzie Bates launched an early barrage of attacking shots against her bowlers – reaching an intimidating 62 for 0 at the close of the powerplay. Gradually, by dexterously and calmly juggling her team's fightback, Knight engineered a crucial repression of any late-scoring spree, as the Vipers' innings drew to a close. Their return, in the last ten overs – 73 for 6 wickets lost – was maybe 20 runs down on what the Vipers might have hoped for and it opened the proverbial door.

With the dramatic removal of Indian batting goddess Smriti Mandhana third ball of the Western Storm innings, Knight was cast into the action prematurely. She found a partner in Priest and then Wilson but when finally joined by Deepti Sharma, Storm needed both the calm of a further combination-effort and some serious wallop. They brough both, triumphantly, in a stirring and tremendously enjoyable finale. What sticks in the memory is that picture of Heather Knight in a prolonged batting zone, where she is serene, controlling but then also bursting out from her previously entirely worthy but possibly limited stature - as a 'steady bat' - into wonderful, potent, effective, liberated new territory. She smashed it, gloriously.

TWENTY-THREE – HEROES.

We go again, with blokes. Freely: un-selfconsciously, if possible. I'll disagree with this tomorrow!

- Dylan Thomas. Pompous Welsh genius who made it okay (I think) to luxuriate in words. Still grappling with discomfort and even anger, over his monstrous lack of care for almost everything... except that need to express, sublimely. Still find the crazy, rebellious, childlike fluency kinda dazzling. So right, or wrong, to set aside the callousness and classy (or class-based) indulgence that Thomas and his circle wallowed in? That **Big Question** looms large for me, here: do we just, can we just judge the work? Is that what we do, with artists - allow ourselves to enjoy, without qualification?
- My Dad, my uncle Ken and The Mighty Vic.
- To a mixed-up, punky youth, Elvis Costello, Paul Weller, John Lydon, Mark E Smith, Joe Strummer plus Bunnymen, Joy Division and many others were genuinely **MASSIVE.** And still probably **are.**
- Slightly later, maybe, Tom Waits joined the sacred posse. Later still, Radiohead, who have been the greatest band of the last 20 years, yes? (Cue bun-fight).
- Books and writing-wise, there have been many things that have touched or inspired me – and still

do. But these people are not feeling like heroes as such. Not today. Not without disproportionate contemplation for this bullet-pointed moment. May be similar for painters but hey, the main reason I'm not going to pump out a list is because it would simply be tooooo pretentious.

- Sports-wise, we're looking at Colin Harvey, Joe Royle, Alan Ball – the early Toffeemen. Matt Tees and Stuart Brace at Grimsby Town. Duncan McKenzie. Alan Hudson. Maybe Teddy Sheringham.
- International heroes or gods (and I get that they *really aren't the same*) would have to include Pele, Rivelino, Luigi Riva, Maradona, Cruyff, Krol – half of that magnificent Dutch team that somehow fell short, in terms of silverware, for a decade or more. Giresse. Bergkamp. Messi.
- In cricket I did love Derek Randall and Michael Holding, and admired Botham and Richards. Rated Hadlee and probably hated Warne but came to respect his achievement. Current faves include Woakes and Stokes and Foakes but this could be something to do with Dylan Thomas. And Moeen.
- Athletics felt big when we were young – possibly because Dad was a strong runner as well as a footballer and so we gorged on everything from David Hemery to Coe, Ovett, Cram and all that. (Incidentally that Hemery and John Sherwood Olympic final is a truly profound early memory. Have no idea if that means something special). Enough. Let's move on.

*

This goes back to football – we are football people, originally. Mighty Vic at Goole Town/Doncaster Rovers/ Grimsby Town and Manchester United. My dad at Macclesfield Town. Two of us lads good enough to play semi-pro. Plus that whole man (or child) hours on the pitch thing. Unreal: every waking moment, playing and practicing. Headers. Left foot. 'Backs and Forwards'.[54] Endless in a way that's honestly unthinkable now. Born twenty years later – within eyeballing range of Wenger, say - and I'm a wealthy young man.

We can dream, eh?

It *was* football, though. Which is why it hurts to be drifting. Much of this book is about what forms us, or informs us and I know that football has been like some crazy matrix through which my peers and I (and I trust, very many of you!) have been borne, caught, or fallen. Sometimes we've giggled, as if in some dark, bouncy circus-net; sometimes we've actually grown. Always, we've been rapt stirringly, in sport.

*

In our distant but imperishable youth, a group of us spent a few days at a military base in Lincolnshire, on a county football training thang. I remember we were warned not to walk round the site on our own, for fear of encountering drunk or hostile squaddies! Most of

---

[54] A simple footie practice. Two small teams playing into the same net: one group defending, t'other attacking. Swap after X goals. We'd play for hours.

what happened is lost in the mists: I recall being on the fringes of a ver-ry useful side, being a lightweight twinkler amongst largely over-developed hunks.

Our coach was *of the times*. He saw me as a luxury player: given that around the same time much of the male universe seemed to view Glenn(da) Hoddle in the same way, I can live with that, then and now. It's true I didn't 'fill out' until I was about twenty-six, or it wasn't until then that I began to dominate games by physical presence - not that I was as a 'unit', of any sort - as well as force of personality. But I had ability and typically, coaches either mistrusted it or failed to see where it might lead.

All this (I suppose) because a) I under-achieved but b) (more importantly) I want to air, through experience, the ludicrously high-blown notion that machismo in its various forms has historically undermined sport more chronically than almost any other phenomenon. My experiences were common to many: seen as 'not tough enough' - possibly with some justification – so cast amongst the subs.

On that camp one particular afternoon stands out. We – Linconshire Under 17s, maybe? - had a practice match against Scunthorpe United. They were struggling, I think, in the league. (The game may well have been something of a punishment: I could be mistaken but recall that they started their entire first team against us). Their manager, Ron Ashman, prowled the touchline, like an especially murderous KGB agent. Some of his players seemed in holiday mode, or possibly mid-rebellion but we were decent and we did have a goal threat. Come half-time, we were 4-0 up.

Ashman went ballistic at his players. It was pretty ugly. Their striker Kevin Kilmore, who would later be a minor hero at GTFC, strolled back onto the park, bearing a wry smile: he actually seemed a decent bloke. We drew 4-4.

End of the game and I remember our coach snarkily asking if "it was quick enough for me?" I'd acquitted myself reasonably well but clearly he thought I needed to scurry a little more wildly about the pitch. Not saying he was scapegoating me but it's stayed with me as an example of shit coaching: unhelpful, undermining, and *actually* a genuinely prejudiced misreading of what happened. I played football under great coaches and great people - at school and in local football – but there were and are a lot of clowns about.

*

To cricket – after all, the majority of you will have been expecting a Cricket Book.

My impressionable years were, I suppose the Botham Years. It was an age of innocence in some respects, a time before the concept of Serious Athleticism landed. This is not to say that there weren't serious athletes; but things were such that one of my favourites - Derek Randall - could be both an outstanding international fielder *and* one of The Most Likely to slide down a drainpipe, on tour. You could get away with stuff; on the pitch and off it. No Twitter: no Insta.

I had mixed feelings about Botham, except when he was dismantling the Aussies. He seemed as bumptious as he was brilliant. There were stories about being disruptive of dressing-rooms wherever he went: I never liked that. But he was special. His bowling was wonderful, often despite injury and almost always despite carrying too much weight. He had something and he knew it: it got him wickets from the lousiest of deliveries... because he was who he was.

Hilariously, my brother was the first reporter on the scene to one of Mr Botham's evening adventures. In Scunthorpe. Beefy apparently had words with another young stag, in an alleyway by a nightclub. (This happened whilst Botham was at Scunthorpe United, where he played up front, with some success, for a short period. Ron Ashman signed him). I think my bro' had also been out on the razz. Botham, of course, is now in the House of Lords. My bro' is yaknow, just in the house.

*

A first great memory of live professional cricket, which remains richly vivid. Aged eleven or twelve, we went on a school coach trip to Lincoln, to watch Surrey play Minor Counties North or East (or both, or someone). Geoff Arnold was bowling but mainly I recall him bawling, shockingly loudly, as he appeals. It was almost scary. It was proper Alpha Male stuff, with Senior Pro thrown in. The guy was marking his territory and daring everyone present – particularly batsmen and umpires – to defy his power and certainty. I have no problem with this extraordinary and plainly impactful projection of himself, now: it's just that *then* it struck a naïve young fella as wow – intense.

He ran in what seemed a long way and the whole wheeling, growling experience seemed threatening. The *volume* in the appeal was somehow the natural extension of something surprisingly hateful. Arnold was a tremendous, skillful seam bowler – I can still picture that sharp movement off the pitch – but he may have introduced me to the idea that professional sport may be a place for Nasty Bastards. That's how he seemed, on that day.

*

Critically, cricket was on the telly and available to us, during this era. There was less international action but that real sense of an event was probably stronger. Would like to see the stats on that but oh; hey; not possible. In terms of things scorched into the memory as truly magical, heroic and blisteringly exciting, I'm drawn back to Michael Holding,[55] bowling at full tilt. Witheringly intimidating and beautiful beyond at the same time. Like life itself being expressed to a rip-roaring maximum.

But it was football, really. As youngsters I don't remember being hugely competitive with my bro's; and I certainly don't sense any fundamental inadequacy in

---

[55] Arguably the most watchable fast bowler of all time. West Indian. God-like but fearsome quick.

terms of the parenting experienced. But get this. Us four lads kinda felt compelled to choose different football teams to idolize. (We all conjoined around the Mighty Mariners, naturally). Dad was Man City, Chris Utd, Jes the Happy Hammers, Simon I think became Leeds – but was less interested. I became fanatical Everton.

How this Toffee Man-ship happened, exactly, I am not entirely clear. Everton were in classic School of Science[56] mode, with Harvey, Kendall, Hurst, Labone so they were good and good to watch. I came to love that midfield – maybe particularly with the addition of Alan Ball – and for years Joe Royle was my god. (I think a guinea-pig may have been named after him: a two-season wonder, inevitably). I wrote off for those exciting-but-dull printed autograph sheets and got a few in person, too.

Everton (then as now?) were highish profile without being uncoolly obvious. Plus they weren't taken. They were magic, to me – despite that infamous Emlyn Hughes chorus[57] – for about twenty years, before the import of the Mighty Vic's involvement at M.U. eased me over to the Red Side. (Now I do follow both, less intensely than in those formative years - which of course means I truly am a Part-time Supporter).

---

[56] Everton acquired this moniker for a tradition of intelligent, tactically-shrewd, dynamic football that felt somehow impressively modern.

[57] Grr. The former Liverpool skipper – after a lorryload of sherberts – infamously and foolishly sang "Liverpool are magic, Everton are tragic, lalaa la-lah", at a particular public celebration.

Digging deep, I'm wondering if I might have been given a blue shirt, early doors? Maybe one of those thick cotton ones with a saggy, white, round collar: one of those general-purpose jobs that might sell to Chelsea/ Leicester/Birmingham City fans? Whatever: the clincher was that Mrs Rawson from up the road stitched a number eight – by this time, for Alan Ball – onto the back of my exotically orange Everton *away shirt*. (Think I had socks, as well. One of the great Christmas presents). Soonish, I went the whole hog and got some white boots; thought I was everything.

I loved Everton, really loved them; cried when City beat them in the FA Cup semi. Tommy Booth goal, City in red and black. Dad cheered, I blubbed - when I was about sixteen. It was **all football**.

*

Dad would occasionally take to us matches. We'd go to the nearest Division One grounds to see our teams. Once we featured on the front page of the Derby Pink;[58] some daft bloke with three of his sons. Think that was an Everton game.

We also went to Forest to see West Ham or United: may have gone to Filbert Street too. Distant, but magical, all that. Seeing Best, Charlton, Law, Byrne, Foulkes under lights, or Bobby Moore. Live. On veg patches, mostly. Cacophonous, exhilarating, manly affairs. Match of the

---

[58] Back in the day many cities had Sat'dee Evening Football Papers – often pink.

Day caught us briefly, once, when Dave Mackay took a throw-in in front of us, at the Baseball Ground. Could weep now, to think that the father who ushered us through those turnstiles was gone before our home club, Grimsby Town, won the Third Division in 1979-80.

*

Best matches include that England v Argentina. Also remember Gunter Netzer waltzing round England, at Wembley: a 1-3 massacre, if my memory serves. And Everton Liverpool Cup semi's - one at Maine Road where McDermott scored with a ridiculous chip - and the Cup Final that Liverpool won 3-1. Everton were magbloodynificent, that day, for best part of an hour. We were (or I was), as they say, *there*.

Other incredibly rich experiences include watching Bobby Robson's England against West Germany in that World Cup Semi: albeit on telly. We were in dreamland for 50-something minutes, watching the most extraordinarily complete performance by an England team that I can ever remember. Then defeat. Numerically, most magic moments were spent in the Pontoon Stand, or possibly the Barrett's, at Grimsby Town FC. Promotions with 20 thousand there. Wins against Everton, scary battles against Chelsea, with their fans ominously strolling along the pitch side and jumping in to ours.

I haven't left football entirely but have drifted. It's going to sound like a generational thing if I blame new-fangled technologies or strikers not striking or the ubiquity of flimflam (whatever that is). Instead, in all seriousness, accepting my relative estrangement, I'll just innocently ask how many think that sport *is* de-valued by fakery and/or cynicism? (O-kaay, know both have been around since the beginning but you understand my meaning). And **does it matter** and/or how much does it matter that say Mourinho and Kane appear to be different shades of shameless? How do we make reasonable judgements on that, when half of us are brain-dead-tribal and the ground culture has one eye on some other timeline?

How *do we* decide? Are we really just Old Farts if we call out The Deceivers? Because it feels to me like winning honestly is better than winning. And seeking to win honestly has value. And it's maddening that even raising this means half the universe thinks I'm the Michael Gove of football punditry.

Despite what talk-shows and phone-ins may suggest I reckon most supporters (of any sport) *strongly prefer* to see their side win in a way that's attractive/exciting/compelling. This implies some understood goodness. It implies something, too, about recognition for those who deserve to succeed. Folks understand the spirit of the game(s) – even if we'd be foolish to call it that, now – and the default position for real supporters is closer to magnanimity than to malice.

*

I would like to believe all that: probably do. But the provocative complexities that come into play here reflect powerful differences in interpretation of values or priorities. One view is that there are universal meanings or truths in sport, which most of us pick up – often intuitively. Because we've been there. Because it's obvious and we feel it. But is that sense of the 'spirit' of things any more legitimate than Fan A bawling "bollocks: gimme da three fakkin'points?"

Tribal phone-ins may reduce these pompous postulations to myopic trash but I'm hoping in the wider world people do know what's fair and good. Which makes me happy enough to suggest that it isn't of itself either 'old-fashioned' or even ill-advised to propose that there will always be a moral component to this. Understanding is part of the love of the game.

TWENTY - FOUR – THINGS I DON'T KNOW.

1. Top level sport: I'm guessing, pretty much. Like zillions of us, I was nearly good enough but not quite.[59]

2. I've never been to Lords. Or, the one time I went it was rained-off. Supposed to see Lancashire in the late Clive Lloyd era. Gay friend of mine was a huge fan; we got into the indoor centre for about three minutes, saw Isaacs batting, I think. So I don't know about Lords.

3. Don't know how it works that Everton could be all over Liverpool in the FA Cup Final at Wembley, in 1986, for an hour, but get beat 3-1. (Actually I do and this is one of the joys of sport. But when you're sat there, in blue, and Everton have been absolutely brilliant and a genuinely classic performance *and victory* looks on, it can be pret-ty bloody challenging

---

[59] Love all this. How many of us in the UK? Say 65 million. Of which 43 mill have been told by their sports teacher that they will play County Cricket. I was, aged about twelve, by Owen Roberts, 'who was never wrong'. Except he was. State Grammar School became Comprehensive – no issue with that - but it meant no cricket from aged 12. Another diamond un-polished.

RICK WALTON

when Jan Molby and Ian Rush suddenly turn up and change history). Incredible day on many levels. Not least for the moving outbreaks of Liverpudlian Unity.

4. How, when he was plainly the best midfielder in Europe at the time and the outstanding French national stars of the era were saying exactly that, was Glenn(da) Hoddle still 'having to prove himself' to England, in about 1983?

5. How did Sam Allardyce get to manage England? And does he really drink pints of wine?

6. How do most school inspectors sleep at night?

7. If I would literally have collapsed, with fear, facing Michael Holding.

Related: how you can *hook* Mitchell Starc – or Johnson! - *after* they've hit you on the helmet? Or how can you watch Brian Close, from about 1578, taking all those body-blows, without curling up in the bathroom and never coming out? Seriously? Playing Holding/Garner/Roberts/Marshall/Walsh or anybody seriously tall and quick takes unthinkable courage, skill and reflex. Cricket balls are hard. They're coming at ninety miles an hour. The bowler is aiming at your ear. Close opted to take the pounding but incredible, zenith-of-Zen/ apex of Alpha Male-ism and remarkable, remarkable focus *to **not turn your back** and instead choose to* actually hit it. *Also*, less scarily but still a legitimate enquiry, how to clip quick bowling – or any bowling - off the legs, like the pro's do? As though there's no possibility they'll ever miss. I miss.

8. Was 1979 the Greatest Ever Year for albums? And/or, for music? Quite possibly. (Go look).

9. How come it's unthinkable for Ordinary People to access visual art – to look at it with comfort and recognise something of its language and power? How did we let that process of exclusion take place?

10. How, no matter the alleged colour of their politics, can endless successive governments fail to see the developmental significance, relevance and depth that sport and activity can provide, in schools? Can you ever remember a Westminster government that genuinely seemed to make the link between sport, well-being, confidence and achievements? And then put their money where that connection was? How is it possible that **even now** there is no central place for P.E/Physical Literacy/kids who express themselves most fully through movement?!?

11. How to score and umpire authoritatively in cricket. Sorry but can't and don't really want to do that.

12. How to conduct oneself with confidence and equanimity around sex and race. How to exclude prejudicial thinking with all that baggage in the attic. All you can do is try. Hard. (I know I'm willing but failing).

13. How, actually, this quietly rebellious jukebox avoided fronting a mighty punky art-schooltastic band, from about 1976 onwards. Could still be a West-Walian Billy Bragg.

14. Where to go to find political and philosophical peace of mind. New Zealand?

15. Why it's not more widely known that the Rugby Community has a ver-ry dim view of levels of sportsmanship in football. (*Thinks*: sportsmanship? Is that even a word I can still use?) In fact, those Premier League Football Legends are regarded as a glove-wearing laughing stock. Set aside issues of class, or snobbery – I know they may be in play. There is a powerful acknowledgement abroad that something is rotten, in football; meaning those pesky moral dimensions are cropping up. (Important to note there is little smugness about this, in my experience. Rugby People are often Football People too... and tend not to be revelling in some noxious superiority. *Also*, rugby at the top end is struggling with the concept of Financial Fair-play – and therefore reeking more of money and inequality than at any time, arguably. So the game is not without issues). But it's not just Nigel Owens who reminds players to maintain standards by saying "we're not footballers". It's *routine* for rugby coaches to call out fakery, arrogance or 'over-celebration' in their games as 'being like football' – and therefore crass. I find this interesting; striking, even.

16. When am I going to know if **all that heading** of a heavy, leather football, often with a 'lace' which was like a dangerously abrasive seam, will takes its toll? Has it already started? My memory feels less complete, less trustworthy. Have few fears but don't relish the prospect of losing my marbles early doors.

17. Is it odd or inadequate in some way to be no great historian of sport? I love it but don't treasure detail – maybe unless it's visual. Plus forget. My knowledge feels authentic but I ain't gonna be able to prove it in your quiz.[60]

18. How – really, how – do you that thing of engaging with people who have ideas that violently repel you? That register with you as prejudice. Because my therapeutic efforts at the end of CHAPTER EIGHTEEN although sincerely meant, may not always carry through with dignity intact. I get angry with people: not often in their presence, but angry. Understand that there may again be dangerous ironies in play if this flawed arsehole talks about his exasperation and resentment in the face of racism, sexism and homophobia but, seriously, how? How do you keep a lid on Righteous Rage? I trigger waaay too early, too often. Which means I duck out, sometimes, when I should be challenging folks. You?

19. Is there a way to read abstract paintings confidently? (And yes I am being specific, here). How do you get to *that place* when let's face it, we're a diabolically visually-illiterate bunch, who probably can't trust ourselves to look and let the art just work on us? I like and may be a little comforted by the idea that this too is a language we can learn but still harbour concerns that *not being able to see* is a cursed but

---

[60] Just me, or anyone else bit turned-off by the neediness and nerdiness around facts/figures/stats? Legitimising. Is it not okay just to love the games?

appropriate judgement on our rank inadequacy as a race. I mean... how much are we looking, really?

20. Who's good with small-talk? How?

21. Why it's kindof generally assumed that 'Mad Ideas' are mad? Because that's what Kandinsky and Keats and Joyce and Pollock and William Webb Ellis had. Is the business of art and invention not predicated on revolution, dissent and/or things that we the great, unthinking unwashed don't get – initially, or ever? And therefore does it not feel that we are living/writing/experiencing crazily unambitiously, with only about twelve percent of our senses engaged?

22. How much are we simply following footsteps? Saw a pic of my Dad, recently (from Hong Kong, about 1962) where he was looking sporty and wearing pretty much the same working/teaching clobber I now wear to the day-job. (Reminder: he died when I was about seventeen - so before I was really computing stuff, you would think). Do have a sense that MY WHOLE LIFE may be about paying homage. You?

23. Is Sky Sports worth it? Or are we gonna need a whole raft of pay-TV Channels, this time next year? What can *you justify,* to the family?

24. I do not know how people can be so wonderful... and yet so stupid. But let's not get back into politics.

TWENTY-FIVE – THINGS YOU DON'T KNOW, MOTHERFUCKER.

1. #Lifesrichwotnots. Although maybe you do now, eh?

2. The lyrics to 'No Birds' - Public Image Limited. '(The) shallow spread(s) of ordered lawns…'

3. That electronic music could be soulful, could have 'heart'. (Witness various things by Human League).

4. The fact that **everything you see, hear and do informs what you do.**

5. (That) Vincent van Gogh's letters, Guillaume Apollinaire's criticism, the crazy-fascist Futurist Manifesto and lots of things wot Grayson Perry says… are as critical to human wellbeing as the artworks themselves.

6. 5. is at least 38 percent untrue but there is some real traction in the idea that (for example) painters write and talk wonderfully about art and life. Therefore *read art books* and learn about art theories as well as go to museums. Erm, what brought this on? Tracey Emin: programme about her and Munch. About their commonalities. Found it interesting, how deep and troubled they both have been/are - how they

both scream, in fact. Emin said something about not going on the defensive about **her decision** *(her obligation)* **to trammel up all her energies towards the moment of making her art.** It sounded kinda lofty but utterly true for her: it was a *statement,* alright. I paraphrase but she was absolutely staring the universe of critics and cynics down as she said 'I am entitled to get into my zone of maximum awareness, to perform my art. That's what proper artists do'. Am I the only one to feel some fabulous and maybe hilariously distant connection with Buttler's "fuck it?" (If I am, fine). Emin, a hugely traduced and misunderstood figure, plants her flag deep and true. She demands respect for that wholeness – that heightened awareness – which is hers as an artist. She understands that wholeness isn't just for her: she's representing the best of us.

7. Coast Path Walks. Ideally wiv pooch.

8. Barcelona. (Except maybe you do). So Martin's Haven.

9. How to get a girl who has 'never done anything' to join with a cricket session. Be friendly. Place a teddy in her arms. Exchange 'passes' with her up and down the sports hall. Listen to her: recognize her. Draw her in with daft jokes and encouragement. Don't make her A Special Case but do make movement possible - *enjoyable, even.* Within weeks she'll be joining a local sports club. (*Fact).

10. How to value a lad who everybody else seems to be pushing away, because he's a 'right handful'. Cut him some slack. Talk and let him talk.

En-bloody-courage. Bring him round to the things he needs to do (in your cricket team) over weeks not minutes. If he can stay with it the cricket team thing might be the single most important positive experience in his life. Everywhere else people are bollocking him. So metaphorically maybe, put your hand on his shoulder. He's worth it and it's right.

11. Guitars. They're easy, really. Plus now with the interwotsits you can learn the words and chords to every song you ever drooled over. Think about it – that's massive. **Learn the chords.** Sing along like a mad idiot. It's do-able; a version is do-able ver-ry soon. (As someone who stopped playing for years – get yourself playing. Get your head and your fingers around **bar chords** and you're made). Or something else musical. N.B. Everything is musical; we're wonderfully wired to react to it – babies in the womb, punks on the floor. Feel for it; you don't have to understand it. I don't understand how 'Treason' joins 'Song From Under The Floorboards', 'Poptones' and 'Life During During War-time' in the Anthems of my Soul pile. It just does, because music just is.

12. Trying like hell to be honest, decent and without prejudice is a lifetime's work. And it's compulsory. We'll all fail but c'mon, let's have a right good go at it.

13. Little kids don't need much. Just some attention and some movement.

14. How good you are at sport doesn't matter.

15. Fleetwood Mac were shite. (Or o-kaay, it was wonderful that two women fronted and wrote all

the songs. But Fleetwood Mac start and finish with musical conciliation: they made punk necessary).

16. We may have been wrong about Ole Gunnar... but maybe not completely?

17. Nothing really changes until we abolish private schooling. It's the source of all privilege: there will therefore be no change. (Note to self: check on whether that twitter-thing about no private schools in Finland was true. Bloody interesting, if so).

18. Living off-grid, in the Canadian wilderness, might be heaven. Living where I do *is,* pretty much.

19. At most sports clubs in the universe, three people volunteer to do the work of ten, and they do it for forty years. They are like gods, to me.

20. Religion is surely ridiculous? Have faith in people – let's get people educated and confident.

21. It's no accident that without over-thinking it, I decided to set up a blog that pretty much alternated sport and art, in July 2011 - bowlingatvincent.com The name itself is supposed to be some weird, witty conflation of cricket and Van Gogh. So sport and art (and I hadn't really thought of this 'til *right now)* have been not just unconscious go-to zones for nourishment or entertainment or something. They've been my public forum. Know what? I like the idea that I've been spewing out heartfelt cobblers on these two subjects for a decade. I started up cricketmanwales.com to cover cricket and kinda support the work mission in March 2015. Both the blogs are wildish, 'expressionistic' and personal.

They are both written in the knowledge that what's being done may not strike everybody or anybody as Proper Writing. Happy to take that risk: have always meant it when I've said that this is just supposed to be a contribution. I hope it's interesting.

22. None of us know – but ain't it great thinking about it? – whether Jos Buttler *actually played better*, having written those two words on his bat handles. (Stats both can and can't cover that). We imagine it may have made him *feel better* but who knows if that's the same thing?

23. None of us know if pressure in sport, in work or in life is real: hey, there are compelling arguments that life itself may not be. But we know what we feel, or we think we do. And pressure feels real. So. Are we escaping or retreating into sport? (And is this good?) Or are we growing, expressing our wholeness more satisfyingly, more completely, through it? I think some of us are. Could be that the planet is knackered and the economy done for *unless* zillions of us develop a positive, life-long relationship with **activity**: really could be. In heart-warming, hysterical teams; solo, competitively, or otherwise; we need to get moving.

24. Maybe it's good that none of us know what the truth is - no matter how sure we feel. Uncertainty is good. Humility is good.

25. You don't know much about the troubles in my heart… and I don't know much about yours. When the time is right, I'll listen: meantimes I really wish you well.

TWENTY- SIX –
A DETERMINATION.

I know some stuff but I love being clueless. (Maybe except when embarrassment strikes; and it does). I know that you don't need to have died in 1564 to be a genius – so leave off with the necrophiliac stuff about tradition and class and hierarchy. Feels like we're neck deep in weird, masochistic subservience and *un-seeing* but if we look, it's undeniable that what the artists amongst us still do, or seek to do, is represent the greatness or find the great secrets within us. And that is astonishing and rousing: death-defying. Perhaps especially when those artists – painters/singers/film-makers – seem ordinary, like us.

If there is meaning to life it surely springs from creativity and from movement – in the physical *and* emotional sense? In my case this means blundering on through sport and art; unable or perhaps disinclined to flawlessly unpick every happening... but being watchful.

*

The recent 'artsy'-philosophical documentaries by Adam Curtis[61] provide a stellar example of almost ecstatically rich human soul-searching. (Waded in there, via BBC iplayer:[62] 'All Watched Over by Machines of Loving Grace' and 'Can't Get You Out of My Head'. Sensational and transfixing ideas-fests, both).

Curtis *investigates*... and then presents his artwork. Some folks are bewildered or politically unsympathetic but the originator has done his job: the oeuvre itself makes clear that Curtis seeks to respond to the universe in his appropriate, individual way, rather than *explaining everything*. I'm with him, in believing in abstraction **and** sense. Surely the crazy-ambitious clamour for everything – for what it's like to be there, be wholly present, be robbed or inspired – is often more human and more true than that which focuses but reaches less?

*

---

[61] Film-maker, radical, philosopher. Has made series of profound, challenging documentaries – he uses the term 'emotional histories' - which break through into a kind of expressionistic art/politics combo. Essential stuff, in my view.

[62] *In passing*: have serious concerns about BBC News and the slide into equivalence or 'balance'. But BBC iplayer really is a treasure – for arts, sports, films, drama, every bloody thing. Scary that yet again it looks as though the Beeb Directorship will be from the Philistine right.

It's not at all clear to me that there is such a thing as High Art but this could be the anarchist breaking through. Why should and why might classical music be intrinsically more valuable than pop, when both can evidence the mind-blowingly profound? If you haven't yet found that two minutes thirty slice of (alleged) ephemera that strikes you as so perfectly eloquent, so intelligent of the human condition *as well as being bloody wonderful to dance to* then what the hell have you been doing all your life? Is it not seriously thrilling to find daft wee songs – and maybe particularly song lyrics - that actually have incredible *integrity?* As though the writers are writing for their lives – for our lives? I find those songs and I find them electrifyingly uplifting.

If I switch crassly across to sport here I'm not thinking this is because I seek equivalents. (Although how can we be sure? I suspect that some of the performance psychology stuff I've read which traces or stresses *trusting the process* and *allowing* that sublime shift into The Zone may confirm some shared essences between mighty artistic expression and sporting performance). But the purpose of this book is not to suggest that. I think the purpose of this book is to suggest interesting things; maybe from experience.

Lots of us can evidence the transforming power of sport. Sometimes it's unhelpfully personal or internal – so not always readable to funders, councils, governments. But it's there, like some wonderful wave, carrying us, weight-bearing our frailties, easing or heaving us forward. I have seen this so many times, in schools or cricket or football or rugby clubs. Girls who 'never do anything' but then do. Boys that are simply unmanageable but then aren't. Teams that pull together because that's simply what happens.

*

There's a fabulous film of Maradona warming up which periodically does the rounds on social media. His pre-game ritual becomes a spectacle and an expression of extraordinary but also bewitchingly casual joy. Sure, he's showing off. Sure, he's warming up. But he's sending signals of greater import out to the universe than just "look out, Dave Watson" (or whoever). The guy's stretching what it means for humans to be coordinated, cool and ready to go. Go where – who cares? The statement stands; has *been registered*, with Mr Watson, forty-thousand in the crowd and with almighty god, if she's watching - which I'm guessing she is. Maradona, we understand, is presenting his offering.

*

I do believe, I think, that coaching is about reading the human; almost as much as about technical knowledge or high-level experience. So these rambles off into artsy stuff are part of my own (low-level) armoury. Coaches need to understand. We need sensitivity not machismo. This of course is not to say that I'm expecting y'all to drop your barbells and go read something about Rothko – although I do recommend it. (The story of the Seagram Murals is like some high-angst version of a fable where Jos Buttler refuses, on moral grounds, to take up his place in The Hundred).

Tactics, toil and yup, the ability to lead are boxes that need to be ticked. Beyond this – and in a sense I do think it *is* beyond - my hunch is listening and judging skilfully are massive, irrespective of competitive level.

*

Sagacious friends I get that many coaches, many people don't lock in to painting or writing or films for the kind of airified nourishment I've been so high-falutingly striking out towards. (And I get that therefore some will be embarrassed at the pretentious guff dancing around my edges, here). But we all grow, we all learn: we **need to**. Sometimes the lessons come to us, especially if the old antennae are twitching in good faith. Maybe this might mean checking out Big Thief; maybe it might be listening to that young lad who's too scared to face quick bowling. Perhaps this is all about trying to *receive* as well as we can?

Ha! In the erm *Psychological Ocean* I'm a Grimsby-born lad cod-fishing way over my depth. This purple nonsense is on somebody else's subject. I merely daub at it to suggest some un-joinable dots. Everything's musical. Everything's corporate. The homeless are sleeping on the lawns.

Until you realise / it's just a story.

YOU HAVE BEEN WATCHING: Rick Walton aka @cricketmanwales aka @bowlingatvinny. Bloggist extraordinaire (or something) at cricketmanwales.com & bowlingatvincent.com

GENUFLECTION:

Finally, thanks again to Paul Mason, Kevin Little, Kate Webb, Paul Hayward, George Dobell, Ian Herbert, Adam Collins, Brian Carpenter and Barney Ronay for their explicit support, plus comradely hugs or handshakes to Dan Norcross and Melinda Farrell for being friendly and generous when I first joined the Cricket Media Posse.

Cheers, you guys!

Rick.

Now one concluding missive, from a fellow (Welsh) cricket man:

I came across Rick Walton as I followed my passions through the sea of words, pictures and videos that is Twitter. His boat floated mine. I was intrigued by his moniker (@cricketmanwales) and attracted by his regular output in relation to his work as a Community Cricket Coach.

I soon realized there is a lot more to Rick than this. He's a bloggist (his preferred description), a champion of elite women's cricket, an offhand, humour-studded philosopher and a lover of much more than sport.

Unfailingly positive, unflinchingly determined to speak his mind on the issues of the day and unnervingly quirky in style, his writing has formed a regular part of my Twitter experience. He wouldn't believe it but I have read more of his blogs than pieces by Jonathan Liew or Barney Ronay.*

He has a voice, both in writing and in actuality which is engaging and enjoyable. Nothing appears to blunt his optimism and enthusiasm. Anyone who has tried to write and get it noticed will know how powerful this is when faced with the universal disinterest that usually accompanies our heartfelt outpourings.

We need more Rick Waltons but, short of that, we should cherish the one we have. Not the only but the first thing we can do is to spend a bit of time reading what he says… and who knows we might just find that he says something that helps us to join the dots in our lives.

Stephen Hedges. Author of 'The Player from Ponty' and CC4 Museum of Welsh Cricket Podcast Presenter.

*Show me the stats! (Rick).

9 781839 75792